Clinton Anderson's
Downunder Horsemanship
Establishing Respect and Control for English and Western Riders

Clinton Anderson's
Downunder Horsemanship

Establishing Respect and Control for English and Western Riders

Clinton Anderson

with
Ami Hendrickson

PHOTOGRAPHY BY
Charles Hilton

ILLUSTRATIONS BY
Caleb Gray

Trafalgar Square Publishing
North Pomfret, Vermont

First published in 2004 by
Trafalgar Square Publishing
North Pomfret, Vermont 05053

Printed in Hong Kong

Disclaimer of Liability
The authors and publisher shall have neither liability nor responsibility to any person or entity with respect to any loss or damage caused or alleged to be caused directly or indirectly by the information contained in this book. While the book is as accurate as the authors can make it, there may be errors, omissions, and inaccuracies.

Library of Congress Cataloging-in-Publication Data

Anderson, Clinton.
    Clinton Anderson's downunder horsemanship: establishing respect and control for english and western riders / Clinton
Anderson with Ami Hendrickson ; photography by Charles Hilton ; illustrations by Caleb Gray.
        p. cm.
    ISBN 1-57076-284-8
1. Horsemanship. 2. Western riding. 3. Horses—Training. I. Hendrickson, Ami. II. Title.
SF309.A52 2004
798.2'3—dc22   2004003154

Book design by Carrie Fradkin
Jacket design by Heather Mansfield
Typeface: ITC Giovanni, Bernhard Tango, Charlemagne, Lucida Sans

9 8 7 6 5 4 3 2 1

WARNING

Equine training can be a hazardous activity, which may subject the participants to possible serious injury. Clinton Anderson and his associates will not assume any liability for your actions.

This book provides general information, instructions, and techniques that may not be suitable for everyone. No warranty is given regarding the suitability of this information, the instructions, and techniques to you or other individuals acting under your directions. Personal instruction, in addition to viewing Clinton Anderson's entire equine video series, is suggested to best understand these training ideas.

Dedication

I would like to dedicate this book to my grandparents, Fred and Thelma Piercy, my parents, Robert and Cheryl Anderson, and my wife, Beth.

Contents

Acknowledgments

No book is possible without the help and support of many behind-the-scenes people.

Thanks to Martha Cook at Trafalgar Square for providing the impetus behind the entire project.

A world of thanks to Charles Hilton for his photographic expertise. And thanks to Caleb Gray for providing such clear illustrations.

Special thanks to Paula Horsch and Cecelia Trabert for being such willing, committed, communicative students.

Personal thanks from Clinton

I have been very fortunate to have worked with true, masterful horsemen. They taught me so much—about horses, about people, and about life. I owe them a huge debt of gratitude.

I would like to thank Gordon McKinlay from Rockhampton, Queensland, Australia. Gordon taught me the importance of getting a solid foundation, doing your groundwork, and preparing the horse before you get on. He is a master at starting unbroken and problem horses. He is a tremendously hard worker and a very honest man. Without the time I spent with him, there would have been a big hole in my life and in my program.

Ian Francis, of Gympie, Queensland, is truly a great trainer. He helped me get my horses soft, supple, and responsive. He excels in many different performance worlds, including the cutting, reining, and pleasure horse industries. He is a remarkable hand; one of the best in the world.

I thank both of these men for spending so many hours to help me achieve my horsemanship goals.

Thanks to my parents, Robert and Cheryl Anderson. Without your support and love throughout my life, I wouldn't have had the opportunity to learn from these two men, and others.

I also thank my wife, Beth. Without your support and help, all the things I am trying to accomplish would be impossible.

Thanks to Gale McCraw for all your hard work and dedication to my business, and for being such a loyal and great friend to Beth and me.

Thank you to Ami Hendrickson for all your hard work and dedication. You put a lot of heart and soul into this project, and it shows.

Thanks to my apprentice Tara Cunningham for helping edit the book and looking at it from a student's perspective. Your work is appreciated.

I am grateful to these people for being by my side. You are only as good as the ones you have around you.

Personal thanks from Ami

Thanks so much, Clinton, for giving me the opportunity to work with you on this project. And thanks to Beth for the hospitality. You run the best "bed and breakfast" in the country!

Thanks to Charles for your wonderful photos, and to Caleb, the great "eleventh hour" illustrator.

Thanks to Terri Gordon, Sheila LeBeau, and Denise Hettig for volunteering so many hours analyzing pictures.

Special thanks to my family for your support through the many long hours I spent sequestered away in my office. To Robert, the most wonderful husband in the world, and Cassandra, for not begrudging me this work during her first year of life. Thanks as well to "Aunt Mel," Grandma and Grandpa—the best babysitters anyone could ask for.

MEET
CLINTON ANDERSON

Clinton and Mindy, his Australian Quarter Horse mare.

If you have seen his TV program, watched his videos, read his articles, or attended his clinics, then you know that Clinton Anderson's techniques can achieve amazing results with almost any horse—even yours!

A native Australian, Clinton has been honing his knowledge and horsemanship skills since he was very young. When he was only fifteen, Clinton left school to begin a series of apprenticeships with some of Australia's best horsemen. He opened his own training facility three years later. At nineteen, he began conducting horsemanship clinics and seminars.

He has successfully competed at the national level in reining futurities and continues to enjoy reining competition.

Clinton believes that all riders can communicate effectively with their horses, regardless of age or experience. He specializes in showing people how to gain their horses' respect, build trust, and improve responsiveness.

Clinton came to the U.S. in 1995. Since 1997, he has trained, toured, and conducted clinics across the country. Huge crowds gather when he shares his insights and training methods at major equine expositions.

In 2001, Clinton launched a weekly training program on satellite television. The program—the first of its kind—features untrained horses and common "real life" problems. It quickly became the network's most popular equine broadcast.

Clinton trains horses and owners and films his many television and video projects at his home in the Midwestern United States. He also travels extensively, conducting clinics and attending many of the major equine events throughout North America.

A NOTE FROM CLINTON

G'day, mate!

When I was a kid in Australia, I bought every book or video I could find on training horses. But it was hard to relate to the trained horse in the book or video when I tried the techniques on my disrespectful horse. Everything in the book or video just seemed to happen instantly. With my horse, it was a different story.

When you try any training technique at home with your horse, he probably won't do things perfectly, at first. That is the point of training. And that is the point of this book.

This book features real horses. Real riders. Real problems. Real solutions.

The featured exercises are based on an understanding of horse psychology. It is essential that you know why horses do the things they do before you try to train them.

You will see a realistic, step-by-step training approach that you can apply to your own horse in your backyard. Throughout the book, you will see each new exercise as it is presented to two riders and their horses. Neither person is a professional rider or trainer. And neither horse has done any of the exercises before. You will also gain first-hand insight from the riders about their difficulties, breakthroughs, challenges, and rewards.

In order for you to get the most from your training time, I suggest that you:

• Read the entire book before trying any of the exercises.

• Take notes.

• Use the buddy system. Training with a friend can be helpful to both of you.

• Re-read the specific section of the book and your notes.

• Fine-tune the exercise with your horse.

• Be willing to commit to the training program and see it through.

I believe these are exercises that everyone—regardless of riding discipline or experience—should learn in order to be safe, gain the horse's respect, and enjoy horse ownership to the fullest. You will be amazed at how quickly you feel the "Downunder Difference" in your horse.

Throughout this book, as an editorial choice for convenience, I've used the word "he" to refer to a horse in general. Using the masculine pronoun was preferable to calling the horse "it." No inherent gender bias in the text is intended!

So let's get started, mate!

Clinton Anderson

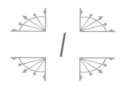

UNDERSTANDING HORSE PSYCHOLOGY

Predators vs. Prey

Everyone who works with horses must understand that horses are prey animals. As prey, horses constantly think that everything in the world is out to get them. Flight from fear has kept them alive for millions of years. If they can't run away, the only option they have is to fight.

A prey animal almost never approaches something directly. If a horse wants to investigate an object, he will walk toward it, making sure there are several escape routes possible. He will approach and retreat until he feels comfortable enough to get all the way up to the object.

People, on the other hand, are predators. When predators want something, they want it *now*. Predators take a direct approach. We will walk right over and get that object.

The problems that arise between people and horses often stem from the fact that humans are predators and horses are prey.

Consider clipping the horse's ears, for example. We know the clippers aren't going to hurt him, so we walk straight up and try to clip his ear. The horse doesn't want us to do this, of course. Our direct approach only makes him more uneasy, but when he tries to escape the perceived threat, we often fight with him. As the situation escalates, the relationship between human and horse disintegrates.

It is very important that you understand this at the outset. Whenever you encounter a problem in your training, your horse is usually just acting like a prey animal. And you, unfortunately, are usually acting like a predator.

Two Parts to Every Brain

A horse's brain has two sections: one is for *thinking* and the other controls *reacting*. The reacting part is big. The thinking part is very small.

The reacting section tells the horse that whenever anything might be a predator, "Run!" The problem is, after the running is

Facing Page

It's never too early to teach a horse to use the thinking part of his brain.

1.1

Running from danger enables the prey animal to stay alive. Allowing the trainer to remove this ability requires an enormous level of trust.

over, horses never start thinking. They usually start eating.

We want to change that. We want to teach our horses to use the thinking side of their brains before the reacting side.

There is only so much space between a horse's ears. As a horse begins to use the thinking section, it gets bigger and bigger. This forces the reacting part to shrink.

A well-trained horse has a big thinking area and a small reacting space. With training, the reacting part gets smaller and smaller, but you will never get rid of it completely. You will never be able to "breed it out." You must always be aware of its existence.

Left and Right Stand Alone

In addition to the thinking and reacting parts, every horse's brain has two sides: *left* and *right*. Each side is separate.

A horse may be used to seeing you on his left side. When he looks at you out of his left

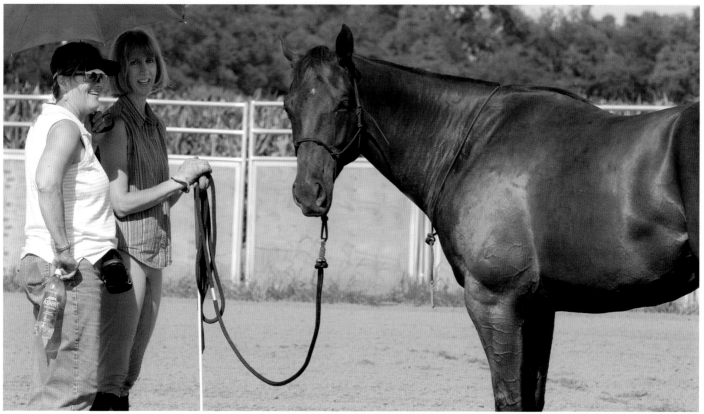

1.2 A–C

A horse's instinct is to react when scared. With enough training, a horse can learn to stop …and think through a situation.

1.3 A & B

Teach each new exercise…   *…one side at a time.*

eye, he allows you to mount him or lead him around. Often, however, if you try these things from the right, you encounter resistance. This is because the horse's right side was never educated. He never learned to respond when he saw someone out of his right eye.

Act as if you own two horses. Every new exercise must be taught twice—once to each side—in order to have a well-balanced, responsive horse.

Balanced Training

On one end of the training scale are the people who beg their horses to do things.

Some people, for example, will stand in front of a horse with a big bucket of grain, trying to load him on a trailer. Sometimes the horse loads to get the treat. Often, he doesn't. At this end of the scale, the owner bribes the

horse. The horse in question is usually quite disrespectful, as well.

On the other end of the scale are the owners and trainers who are too forceful with their horses. You might have gone to a horse show and seen three or four guys beating a horse to get him to load. They try to push the horse on the trailer. They use ropes and pulleys and winches—and loading the horse becomes a big ordeal.

Even if these people end up getting the horse loaded, sometimes they still lose. The horse could be injured in the process. He may run over or kick someone. Or, he may finally get on the trailer, and then panic, thrash about, and wreck it.

Even if no one is hurt, the problem remains. The horse still doesn't willingly load. The horse on this end of the scale is often

1.4
A well-trained horse is a willing partner.

afraid of his owner. He may also be defensive, because he knows that everything is going to end in a fight.

Ideally, we want to be in the middle of this training scale. We want to be somewhere between the wimp who gets dragged all over the paddock and the aggressive owner who forces the horse to do something.

Unfortunately, wanting to stay in the middle doesn't mean we can. The middle of the training scale is like a line drawn in the sand. If my horse is disrespectful toward me, I step toward the harder side of that line. Once I get his attention and he tries, I can jump back to the easier side.

Our goal as trainers is to stay in the middle. But we need to adjust to the situation, depending on how our horse responds to us.

What Horses Want

You will be more effective at communicating with your horse if you know what he wants.

Horses desire four basic things: *safety, comfort, food,* and *stimulation.*

SAFETY AND COMFORT

Above everything else, horses want to feel safe. Because there is safety in numbers, horses often don't want to leave the barn or their herd mates. If a horse doesn't feel safe, his first inclination is to run away from what frightens him.

A horse must feel safe and certain that nothing will hurt him before he relaxes and feels comfortable.

FOOD

Like all living things, horses need food and water to survive. A horse doesn't eat, however, if he doesn't feel safe and comfortable. If you try to load a horse and he doesn't feel safe or comfortable about being on the trailer, all the food in the world won't change the situation. That is why bribing a horse with food isn't very effective.

STIMULATION

When horses have enough food and water, they need stimulation. Keep things interesting. An interested horse will pay more attention and put more effort into what you ask of him.

Gordon McKinlay, the great Australian horse trainer, once told me that horses need three things—long rides, wet saddle blankets, and concentrated training—in even doses. When these three elements are balanced, your horse benefits from balanced mental and physical stimulation.

Make the Right Thing Easy and the Wrong Thing Difficult

Once you understand these four basic desires—safety, comfort, food and stimulation—you can apply them to your training.

Horses learn through comfort and dis-

comfort. When the horse does what you want, make him feel comfortable. Make him feel safe. Let him know that respecting you won't hurt him. If the horse doesn't do what you want, find a way to make things uncomfortable for him. In other words, make the right thing easy and the wrong thing difficult. Let me give some examples.

If you ask a horse to move and he lazily refuses, distracting him with something new can make him uncomfortable, since prey animals perceive all new things as threats. You could wave a plastic bag up and down. You might be twenty feet from the horse, but he will still get uncomfortable. More than likely, he will choose to move.

Taking a horse's air away can also make him uncomfortable. If you have a horse that tends to speed up more than you want, move his feet and continuously change directions for a while. Soon, he will be "out of air" and want to stop. If you keep him moving, air becomes a valuable commodity. When you say "stop" and let the horse rest, you give him back the air he needs. A little bit of discomfort teaches the horse to have greater respect for you. Suddenly, stopping becomes something he *wants* to do, and you can end a very bad habit.

Many people, however, feel that reward is the only part to training a horse. If you only use reward to teach your horse, you may get him to do what you want, but the result will be an inconsistent horse. Reward is only 50 percent of the equation. If you never make your horse feel uncomfortable for wrong behavior, nothing motivates him to stop making the mistake.

Applying the principles of comfort and discomfort enables you to use the horse's

When the horse responds correctly and yields to halter pressure, the discomfort immediately vanishes, rewarding him.

priority system in order to get the response you want.

When you ask a horse to do something and he refuses—he doesn't even try—motivate him by making him feel uncomfortable in a small way. Then, build the pressure to a level where you are effective and the horse begins to respond in a positive way. Start gently. Increase the pressure gradually, but be effective.

As the horse progresses in his training, you will find yourself rewarding him more and more. You will also spend less time making him feel uncomfortable for doing things you don't want. But, you must always be prepared to step across the line from reward to correction when necessary.

2

THE VALUE OF RESPECT

Defining Respect

A respectful horse is a willing horse. When you ask him to move, he instantly moves. When you walk, he walks with you like a shadow. When you go to his stall in the morning, he comes to you. He wants to be your partner.

Every time your horse pins his ears back, tries to kick you or bite you, steps on your foot, or pushes you out of his way, he is being disrespectful. Many people won't let another human take advantage of them. But they will allow a half-ton animal to push them around.

For every horse that is abused by his trainer (and we definitely don't condone that), there are many more horses out there, abusing their owners. Most horse owners don't even realize they are being abused, which only makes things worse.

Respect is a Choice

We all want our horses to like us. We don't want to make them feel uncomfortable. If your horse doesn't look to you as a leader, however, then he won't want to hang around you. Remember, you never make your horse feel uncomfortable unless he does something wrong or he doesn't try. It is always *his* choice.

This is the same logic horses use with each other.

Carry a big bucket of grain out into a pasture with two broodmares in it and see what happens. The mares don't share. They decide who gets the grain and who doesn't. Eventually, the dominant mare will get the grain to herself. But she doesn't run in and start kicking. She comes in with a system. She uses a step-by-step way—beginning with pinning her ears back and ending with biting or kicking—to let the other mare know that as long as she stays and eats, she will feel uncomfortable (fig. 2.2).

2.1

A respectful horse enjoys being with you.

2.2

A dominant horse commands respect from the herd.

If horses do this to each other naturally, why not use the same method when we want them to learn something? It makes sense to train them using an approach they already understand.

Friendship is Built on Respect

In general, the more you spoil your horses, the less they respect you. If you only love them, pat them, and feed them, but never ask them to respect you or move out of your personal space, they will never believe that you are equipped to lead them (figs. 2.3 A & B).

Soon, these horses don't appreciate anything that is done for them. They begin believing they control the situation. They want to spend less and less time with their owners, who they perceive as weak. The owners want to treat a 1000-pound animal like a big pet, but they don't understand that friendship without respect is dangerous. Many situations—jumping a fence, walking along a busy road, or work-

2.3 A & B

A lack of respect can be dangerous…but cooperation feels good.

ing cattle—rely on the horse respecting your judgment in order to keep both of you safe.

I'm not saying that you can't give your horse a treat or that you can't love him. Of course, you can. And you should. A treat is useful when you have already taught certain behaviors and you want a reinforcement for a job well done. Just remember that treats are a bonus. They are not bribes or payoffs.

Gaining Respect

If you don't earn your horse's respect, everything you want to teach him will be a waste of time. Gaining your horse's respect is not difficult. You get respect when you move your horse forward, backward, left and right, and always reward the slightest try.

You need to be like a dominant brood-mare. If she wants to eat at the hay feeder, she walks in and pins her ears back. The other horses scatter—going forward, backward, left and right—because the boss came in and said, "Move!" They move because the mare has previously shown them that she can drive them out of her space.

If your horse does not respect you, you won't be able to train him well. You will be like a schoolteacher with a class full of kids who are daydreaming, goofing around or talking with each other. You could be the greatest teacher in the world, but the information you give will not be retained. Only when your students pay attention and look at you with two eyes will the lesson sink in.

2.4 A

The more your horse realizes you can control where his feet go, the more respect he will give you.

Follow the Leader

The thought of purposely making their horses uncomfortable bothers some people. They don't realize that, in many ways, a lack of leadership makes their horses uncomfortable.

Your horse wants a leader. He wants to follow somebody. If you are not willing to do the job, the horse will eventually step up to the plate and do it himself. When that happens, you have no control. Your horse has control of you. It can quickly reach the point where it can become physically extremely dangerous for you to be around him.

Gaining the horse's respect doesn't mean whacking him for no reason. If you start thumping on him with a big stick, you won't have respect, you'll have fear.

This book contains a series of exercises, both on the ground and under saddle, that demonstrate to your horse how you deserve the leadership position. Each exercise reinforces the basic principles of moving your horse's feet forward, backward, left and right.

Under no circumstances will your horse follow you, or want to be your partner, if you show any signs that you are not a competent leader. You have to prove to your horse that you are worthy of the job (fig. 2.4 B).

A Reaction Waiting to Happen

Every day, your horse will have a slightly different response to you. Some days, he may feel flighty and jumpy (fig. 2.5). Other days, he may be a bit lazy and lethargic.

How your horse reacts on a given day will determine what you do with him. If your

2.4 B
Once you gain your horse's respect, he will gladly let you lead.

horse acts disrespectfully, do whatever is necessary to get him to pay attention and respect you while you are still on the ground, then continue the lesson under saddle. If your horse is listening to you from the beginning, you probably don't need to spend much time on groundwork that day.

Horses have distinct personalities. Some will challenge you on a daily basis. Others won't. No horse is static and unchanging. Since the reacting part of the horse's brain is always present, every horse has the potential for unpredictability.

Professional People Trainers

Horses are phenomenal "people trainers." We will make up the most ridiculous excuses for the things our horses have trained us to do. We will say, "I can't ride with you because my horse doesn't like your horse." Or, "I can't go on this trail because at the end of it, there's a big ditch, and my horse spooks at ditches." Or, "I can't use this saddle because my horse doesn't like this color." Or, something equally silly.

We must learn to stop making excuses for why our horses don't listen. It's simple: our horses don't listen because we haven't gained their respect. It all starts with you.

You must be willing to say, "I will change. I will learn the steps. And I will be consistent." If you don't say those things and follow them through, all the wishes and hopes you may have for a well-trained, responsive horse will be for nothing.

2.5

*A horse is a reaction
waiting to happen.*

No Shades of Gray

Horses learn very quickly if we make the right thing easy and the wrong thing difficult. Be very clear about what behavior is and is not acceptable. The clearer you are, the faster your horse will learn. Be black and white; no shades of gray.

A shade of gray is inconsistency. It's a place where your horse doesn't know whether he is right or wrong. Any time a shade of gray exists, you set your horse up for failure. Unclear cues and inconsistent training only confuse him.

Many training methods are shades of gray. Sometimes, people nag ineffectively and allow the horse to ignore them. They may release the pressure of a cue at different times. They may take a horse's disrespect personally and allow emotion to cloud their training judgment. Or, they might allow a horse to crowd into their personal space without correcting him.

A shade of gray means, "I'm not really sure." You must be clear and confident—black and white—for your training to be effective.

Be Black or White

The more black and white you are, the faster your horse will learn what you want. Strive for a definite difference between, "That's it! Good boy!" and, "Get out of my space! Stop pushing into me!"

If the horse isn't responding correctly, the faster you can make him feel uncomfortable for that behavior, the faster he will change it. The sooner you can make him feel comfortable when he tries to do the right thing, the sooner he will learn.

For example, let's say your horse pins his ears back and acts as if he will bite you. You must be very clear—black and white—that you will not accept that behavior. If you do nothing, or make a half-hearted correction, you essentially tell the horse, "I want you to bite me next week."

On the other hand, if you immediately react when the horse nips—you might back him up, or do something else to make him feel uncomfortable—he will instantly connect his action with your reaction.

If my horse acts disrespectfully toward me, I will make him uncomfortable very quickly. I will be effective. Then it will be over and done with.

Body Language

Horses communicate primarily through body language. Every time you see them pin their ears, cock their hind leg back, sigh, lick their lips, or open their mouth, they are using body language to communicate different things.

When working with your horse, pay attention to what you say non-verbally. Consistency is key. Be able to change your body language quickly. Use aggressive body language when your horse misbehaves. Instantly relax when he does the right thing (figs. 2.6 A–C).

Assert Yourself

When teaching people to work with horses, I find that many have problems learning to change their body language from *passive*, when the horse is doing something correctly, to *assertive* when the horse is not listening.

Some people can be a little too aggressive. They are often overly demanding and don't give the horse a chance to understand what is being asked. I try to tone down most aggressive people. I tell them to relax a little bit more. Give the horse a chance. Don't be so quick to correct a situation.

Other people have trouble asserting themselves, driving the horse out of their space, or showing with their body language that they are not happy.

I try to light a fire under the passive people. I ask them, "Are you tired of this behavior? Then show me something that tells your horse he did the wrong thing."

You know whether you have a tendency to be overly aggressive or excessively passive. If

"Go forward."

"Stop."

2.6 A–C
Horses are experts at reading body language.

"Come to me."

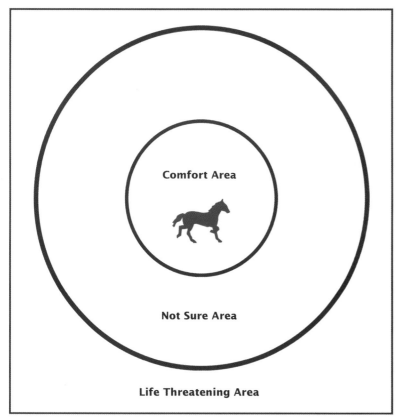

Comfort Area

Not Sure Area

Life Threatening Area

2.7
A horse is happiest in his "comfort area."

you tend to be aggressive, look for opportunities to relax and reward your horse more. If you know you are a bit timid, allow yourself to get tough when necessary.

You can learn to fine-tune your body language. You can walk forward aggressively and communicate, "Move out of my space!" with authority. When the horse responds, immediately relax. You will be amazed at how quickly he understands.

Resistance is Normal—Expanding the Bull's Eye

When working with horses, it is important to remember that resistance is very normal. Whenever you try to teach your horse something he is not used to, you can expect some resistance. Often, the reason for resistance is related to the horse's desire for safety and comfort.

Imagine a bull's eye on a target. In the middle of this bull's eye is your horse. The area around the bull's eye is his *comfort area* (fig. 2.7). He is comfortable and familiar with everything that goes on in that area. Around the comfort area is the *not sure area*. It is full of anything the horse doesn't normally do.

On the outside of the not sure area is what I call the *life-threatening area*. In this place, the horse thinks he is in serious danger. Here, he kicks, bucks, bolts, and rears up over back-

2.8

Taking the horse into the "not sure area" in a controlled way eventually results in an expanded region of comfort.

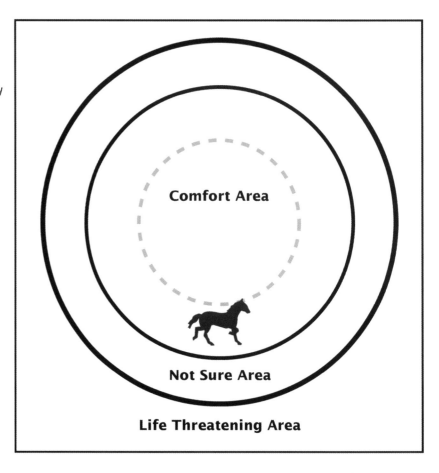

ward. In the life-threatening area, the reacting part of the horse's brain takes over. This area is home to all the really dangerous things horses can do.

We want our horse's comfort area to expand. We want him to be comfortable with a wide variety of things. In order to do that, we have to take him into the not sure area (fig. 2.8).

At first, many things—saddles, ropes, cars, dogs, plastic bags—will take your horse out of his comfort area. Once he enters the not sure area, he probably won't want to do whatever it is you are asking him to do. This is *resistance*.

Have patience. Continue doing whatever you did to bump the horse out of his comfort area. As soon as tries, or improves even a little bit, let him come back to his comfort area. Every time the horse takes a trip out to the not sure area, only leaving it when he has learned something, his comfort area in the middle of the bull's eye grows a little bigger (fig. 2.9).

Don't Quit Before the Try

Any time you take your horse out to the not sure area, you must wait until he tries to figure out what you want before allowing him to go back to the comfort area.

2.9

As the "comfort area" grows, it takes more effort to take the horse into the "not sure area." He will become quieter and easily accept many more things.

If you allow the horse to leave the not sure area before he responds in the right way, you actually teach him the wrong thing. In this case, the comfort area shrinks. It gets tighter and tighter until your horse has a panic attack about everything he encounters.

To build your horse's trust and confidence, it is very important to keep him outside of his comfort area until he begins to try to do what you want.

Any time you begin a new exercise, establish a starting point. The starting point is the simplest place you can begin training and have the horse understand what you expect of him. Many people choose starting points far beyond their horses' capabilities. When they

encounter problems in training, they have no base of understanding to return to.

Every horse has a different starting point for every exercise. It is important to analyze your horse and try to find a basic starting point for him. For best results, start small and work your way to more advanced exercises. If you establish a good starting point you always have a place to go back to if your horse becomes confused during the training process.

Remember: resistance is normal. The majority of people quit training far too early in the lesson. They need to remain patient and work through the resistance. They don't have to get more aggressive or lose their temper. Training isn't about emotion. It is about finding an appropriate starting point and getting the horse to try.

2.9 A & B
Resistance is normal. Train until the horse tries.

How seriously you take responsibility for clear, consistent cues is directly related to your horse's responsiveness to you and respect for you.

As soon as the horse starts to try, stop and reward him. Soon the horse will learn that the more he resists you, the longer he will feel uncomfortable. He will also know that every try is rewarded.

Safety First

Putting pressure on your horse pushes him into the not sure area. But don't pressure him so much that he goes into the life-threatening area. Once your horse is in the life-threatening area, he is too afraid to think. Then you are in real trouble. This area is dangerous to your health, and to the horse's well-being.

At this point, experience and knowledge play a part. You must know when to back off before your horse panics and when to keep going until he learns.

Responsibility Breeds Respect

You have responsibilities, and your horse has responsibilities.

Your responsibility is to be black and white—to make training easy for the horse to understand (fig. 2.10). Whenever you are a shade of gray, you are unclear or inconsistent, which is unfair to your horse.

Your horse has a responsibility to respect you. He may not always do everything right, but he should try to figure out the answer. A disrespectful horse doesn't try. He doesn't care. He is only concerned about what *he* wants and what you can give him.

Though both trainers and horses have responsibilities, it all starts with us.

3

WHO'S WHO

The two riders featured in this book were chosen from hundreds of applicants. Neither of the riders or their horses had ever attended one of my clinics, and the horses had never been taught any of the Downunder Horsemanship® training techniques.

I selected an English rider, Cecelia, and a novice Western rider, Paula, in order to illustrate how each exercise can apply to a variety of riding disciplines.

I also wanted to make sure that the horses our riders used weren't perfect. Both horses had some behavioral problems that are all too common. They bucked under saddle. They were pushy on the ground. They didn't have much respect for their owners.

After each exercise, Cecelia and Paula share their experiences. They tell you how their horses responded, what made sense, what proved difficult, and explain how mastering the exercise affected their mounts.

You will spend quite a bit of time with these ladies in the following pages. It is only fitting that you get to know them a bit first.

Introducing Our Riders...

Cecelia

Cecelia Trabert has been crazy about horses for as long as she can remember. She bought her first horse with her first paycheck thirty years ago. Horses continue to be an important part of her life.

She lives on a farm near Kansas City, along with her husband, Tim, and teenaged son, Jake. They share their farm with five horses (all hunters), a goat, their two dogs, Lucky and Dot, and assorted barn cats, fish, and turtles.

Several equine affiliations count Cecelia as a member. These include the Mid-American Combined Training Association, United States Equestrian Association, United States Dres-

3.1
Paula (left) and Cecelia (right) after an intensive week of learning.

sage Federation, and the American Quarter Horse Association. She is also an active member of the Fort Leavenworth Foxhunt Club and the Kansas City Dressage Society.

Paula

Paula Horsch, her husband, Shaun, and her two sons, Tyler and Cody, live on a small farm in Kansas, near Wichita.

When Paula met her husband, she misunderstood his last name and announced, "I love horses!" Three Paint Horses (and a foal on the way), two rabbits, and a German Shorthair Pointer, named Guss, are all part of the Horsch family.

"I have a wonderful family and my dream home," Paula says. "I couldn't ask for anything more. I sure have been blessed and I am thankful for it every single day."

Paula belongs to the American Paint Horse Association, the Pinto Horse Association, and is a member of the Cheney Saddle Club. In addition to working with her horses, she enjoys spending time outdoors, swimming, water skiing, and camping.

... and Their Horses

Smacks

Early News Edition (a.k.a. "Smacks") was born and bred on Cecelia's farm. Smacks is an Appendix Quarter Horse. His sire is a World Champion, National High Point Stallion, and Congress High Point Stallion. His dam is a Thoroughbred hunter.

From his first introduction to a halter, Smacks has shown a negative attitude when asked to do something that isn't his idea. Several professional trainers have worked with him, with moderate success.

Smacks bucks unpredictably. He has unseated seasoned riders several times. He has a long, sordid history of acting out when trailer loading. He doesn't stand well for mounting and has a habit of tossing his head or stretching his neck out to keep his rider from collecting the reins. Steering and softness are issues, as well. As Cecelia says, "He has moods. I never know which horse I have to ride."

Smacks is five years old. He stands just over 16 hands tall. Cecelia has high hopes for him in the dressage arena. First, however, she needs to find a way to connect with his mind and make him a willing partner.

Fancy

Paula's mare, Ima Fancy Dancer ("Fancy"), is a registered Paint Horse. Fancy is five years old and stands about 15 hands. Her sire is a World Futurity Finalist in Junior Western Pleasure, a four-time Pinto National Champion, and a two-time Reserve National Champion.

After Fancy spent two-and-a-half months with a professional trainer, she still had behavioral problems that intimidated Paula.

Fancy has a history of bucking when asked to canter, both under saddle and on the lunge line. She is difficult to bridle and pins her ears back when being mounted. The mare also tends to be pushy and disrespectful on the ground.

Paula envisions showing Fancy in halter and pleasure classes, but before that can happen, she needs some tools to gain her horse's attention, respect, and cooperation.

Life "B.C." (Before Clinton)

Cecelia's Story

"I showed gaited horses throughout the Southern states for several years. I rode to several state championships and two third place finishes at the World Celebration in Amateur Pleasure classes. When I moved to Kansas, I got bitten by the jumping bug. I joined the Fort Leavenworth Hunt Club in 1993 and have been an active member ever since.

"I enjoy competing in dressage, combined

Paula's horse, Fancy

training, and hunter shows. I currently compete at First Level dressage and Training Level combined training. One of my long-term goals is to move up several levels in dressage. I fantasize about riding Prix St. George.

"From the beginning, Smacks has been difficult about everything. When he was just a month old and already fighting the halter, I remember hoping that wasn't the way he handled new experiences. But so far, he has been difficult about all new things. It is wearing me out.

"I have never been around a horse that is so pushy. Smacks approaches everything with the word, 'No.' For two years, we worked on ground manners. I did everything you are supposed to do with a baby, introducing him to blankets, grooming, having his feet handled, lungeing, and leading. Every new thing met with resistance.

"When Smacks was two, I was successful in loading him in my trailer, along with my wonderful Quarter Horse mare. After standing calmly for about ten minutes, Smacks erupted! He broke the breakaway tie and the butt bar and barreled out the door. I tried every loading technique I came across, but nothing worked.

"Finally, in a last ditch effort, I called a man who is known in the area for taking on serious training problems. He is the one you call before you call 'the killers.' He fought Smacks for over an hour-and-a-half before finally getting him in the trailer—winching him in on his side!

"Smacks spent a month doing 'old-time, cowboy camp' with this man. I was a basket case, but he did learn to load in a trailer and work under saddle.

"As a four-year-old, Smacks went to my dressage trainer for schooling. She went 'nuts' over his trot, but had less than glowing reports about his attitude. She told me that he was stubborn and approached things negatively. I rode him for a while, thrilled at our progress. Then my trainer moved to Florida. Smacks came home… and discovered that he could buck me off and get out of work.

"I try to work Smacks every day. Our routine usually encompasses an hour or more. After grooming and tacking up, I lunge Smacks in side reins for about fifteen minutes, to warm him up. I lunge him at all three gaits. This is my time to check out his way of going, determine what is happening in his little pea brain, and see what I have to look forward to. The lungeing is part of our workout regardless of where I ride. I don't mount up until Smacks relaxes.

"If we work in an enclosed area, I'll generally begin with a series of walk-halt transitions. Once I think we are working well together, I move to walk-trot transitions. I work a lot on bending, steering, and softening. We do serpentines, change rein, do 15- and 20-meter circles, and work on transitions at the walk and trot. These rides usually last thirty to forty-five minutes. I finish our ring work with big trot extensions, if the day has gone well. If the day has not gone so well, we work on serpentines at a walk, doing lots of steering with the seat and legs.

"I am not comfortable cantering him right now. His violent bucking episodes have taken my confidence away. Even though I have been able to stay on him in the past, I am dealing with a big wall of fear.

"When trail riding, I never know what he will do. I only ride with others present. He may be going fine, and then—out of the blue—

he will explode with a huge buck. He becomes rough and resistant when heading back from a trail ride. It is unnerving; like riding a ticking bomb.

"So here I am. I have spent five years hanging in there on a horse that people have said I should give up on. So far, I have been fortunate enough to stay with him, but I hate the uncertainty of every ride.

"I am hoping that some of the sessions I have seen Clinton do will help us. I need something to help me control my horse and stop his outbursts safely. It may be that this is a horse I cannot ride successfully. But I want to give us the opportunity to work things out."

Paula's Past

"I have only been riding horses for about a year-and-a-half. I have taken lessons from a local instructor and ask friends and family for help when I need it.

"In the past six months, my riding confidence has really been broken. I have been bucked off of two different horses. Both were supposed to be gentle. In fact, the word 'bombproof' comes to mind.

"I bought my mare, Fancy, six months ago, on New Year's Eve. The people I bought her from were honest with me. They told me she was green broke and did not have a lot of riding time on her. They also admitted that they were afraid of riding her. Dummy me—I thought I would put thirty days of training on her and everything would be fine.

"Since I am so green at riding, I didn't have any business buying a green horse, but I just loved her.

"Fancy went to a trainer in March. Shortly afterward, he called to say that she had blown up on him and started bucking. Two-and-a-half months later, she was still doing the same thing.

"I saw the trainer ride her in the round pen. When he asked for a lope, she made it halfway around the turn, and then went to bucking. Big bucks! The kind with her back arched and her head down like she meant business.

"When we brought Fancy home, I was afraid. My husband (who is greener than the horse!) said he would ride her. He saddled her up one evening but hadn't even gotten on her before she started to buck.

"After seeing her buck for the trainer and for Shaun, I was scared to death of being bucked off. I didn't work up the nerve to get on her until just three weeks ago. (I figured I have to ride her a *little bit* before taking her to meet Clinton.)

"Our rides only last about five minutes. I have someone hold her when I get on because she lays those ears back like she is getting mad. Then I have someone walk her around, leading her with a lead rope for a while. If she is quiet, I will ride her without being led. I'll practice neck-reining and turning at a walk. I'm afraid to try much more.

"I am a nervous rider now because I am constantly waiting for the horse to startle and jolt into a bucking spree. I am a horn-holder and am scared to lope. I am hoping to get through all that with Clinton's help. I have this vision of coming back a changed, confident rider; no more horn-holding."

How We Got Involved

✳ Cecelia

"I discovered Clinton when I found RFD-TV on the satellite dish. It has been my main channel ever since.

"I saw him trailer-training a horse and was overwhelmed with his results. I started watching every program he did. I was having nightmares about my horse, to the point where my husband and I were considering putting him down. Watching and listening to Clinton made us put off that decision, for which I am very glad.

"I attended Equifest in Wichita, in March of 2003. My friends and I went specifically to watch Clinton (and, of course, to benefit from the other speakers).

"During one of the sessions, there was an announcement that Clinton was looking for a Western and an English rider for a book project. I told my friends I was going to be in the book. They laughed, but I trotted over to the booth, wrote my story, had my picture taken, and stuffed the ballot box with my name. I really wanted to do this!

"I am looking forward to learning from Clinton. I want to be able to have my horse listen to me and respect me. I want to have my horse trot right into the trailer like I have seen Clinton's do and amaze my friends! I want to absorb as many tools, exercises, and concepts as possible. I want the confidence to school my horse correctly and get past this block we have between us."

✳ Paula

"I first met Clinton at Equifest, an equine event held at the Kansas Coliseum in Wichita.

"My farrier had told me about RFD-TV and mentioned that the station featured shows on horse training. I caught an episode of Clinton's and was very impressed. When I saw that he was scheduled to be at Equifest, I took a day of vacation to make sure that I saw his segment.

"I was amazed at what Clinton did with the horse he had. It was a horse he didn't even know. He had that horse acting so differently in only one hour. I went back the next day just to see him.

"When I heard that he was working on a book and looking for someone 'not too experienced' with a horse 'that was a bit too much for them,' I filled out an application.

"When I learned that Clinton had chosen Fancy and me to help him with this project, I couldn't believe it! To me, this is a chance of a lifetime, and I am treating it as such.

"I want to learn as much as possible from Clinton. I plan on getting my horse out of her bucking habit. I want to gain confidence in my riding ability. And I want to learn training techniques that will help me get control of all of my horses and not be so afraid of them all the time."

4

GROUNDWORK TOOLS

The right tools make all the difference when working with horses. Of course, there is no "magic wand" that will make all training easy. Much of the success you have with any training aid is directly related to the time you spend with your horse and the knowledge you bring to the training session.

Every combination of horse and trainer is different. In my experience, the training aids mentioned here help to "level the playing field." I find that they work exceptionally well for people and their horses. They make it easier to be specific with my instructions. They are relatively inexpensive and easily adaptable to many training situations.

You can certainly obtain good results using a wide variety of training tools. You may prefer to use different tools, but it may take a bit longer to achieve your goals.

The following list specifies the training aids I prefer to work with.

Halter

I use a rope halter for all aspects of horse training. Flat, nylon web or leather halters are very easy for the horse to lean on. They give little incentive for the horse to stay light and responsive.

A rope halter focuses pressure over a small area. This makes it less comfortable for a horse to pull against you. Used correctly, a rope halter teaches the horse to yield to pressure, rather than lean into it. Ideally, the halter has two knots on the noseband. These act as pressure points and serve to get the horse's attention if he tries to ignore and lean against you.

A rope halter is easily adjusted to raise or lower the noseband as needed. The lower the noseband, the more leverage and control you have of your horse's head (figs. 4.1 A–C).

14-Foot Lead Rope

When working with horses, a 14-foot rope eliminates the need for separate lead and

Facing Page
Tying a rope halter
(see p. 32)

How to tie a rope halter:

Pull the halter behind the horse's ears and thread the end through the loop on the left side, as shown.

Wrap the end one time counterclockwise around the loop. Thread the end between the loop and the beginning of the counterclockwise wrap.

The loose end points toward the horse's rear, away from his eye.

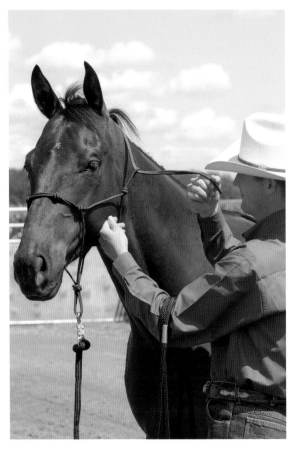

lunge lines (fig. 4.2). It can be used for most groundwork exercises, as well as for everyday leading, lungeing, and tying purposes.

I use a lead of high-quality yachting rope. A heavy-duty, quick-release snap attaches the rope to the halter.

The exercises that follow occasionally refer to various parts of the lead rope.

The *shank* is the portion of the rope between your hand and the snap, approximately four feet from the clip.

The *tail* is the part of the rope at the opposite end of the shank.

4.2

To hold the rope for most groundwork exercises, open your hand with the palm facing the ground. Place the rope in your palm so your thumb is toward the tail end. Your little finger should be closest to the snap.

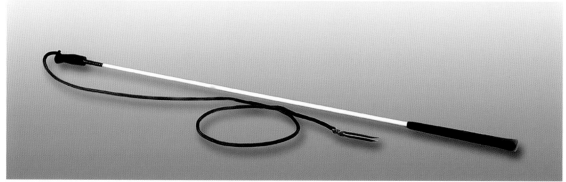

4.3

The Handy Stick and string.

Handy Stick™

The Handy Stick is a four-foot-long, heavy-duty, fiberglass shaft that serves as an extension of your arm (fig. 4.3). It is useful for cueing the horse while maintaining a safe distance. Using the Handy Stick allows shorter handlers to have access to any part of their horses.

The Handy Stick is less flexible than a traditional dressage or driving whip. The added stability makes it easier to control the end of the Handy Stick. The Handy Stick makes it easy to apply specific pressure in easily controlled amounts, lending itself to many desensitizing exercises. A looped, leather tip on the

end can be threaded with a lightweight string. This gives the handler even more "reach" and aids when teaching the horse to relax to ropes and moving objects. A plastic bag affixed to the leather tip is also an effective desensitizing tool.

The Handy Stick is black and white, reminding people to be black and white—no shades of gray—in their training methods.

Most of the groundwork exercises require you to hold the Handy Stick in one of two ways: the *handshake hold* or the *ski pole hold* (figs. 4.4 A & B).

Drive line. Tie the string around the base of the horse's neck just above the shoulder. Use the drive line as a visual reference for a variety of exercises where it is important to position a cue for correct impulsion.

Guide line. Tie the string around the middle of the horse's neck, halfway between the jaw and the shoulder. Use the guide line as a reference for correct position when practicing leading exercises.

String

The string I prefer is a sturdy, thin, 6-foot rope with a loop at one end. It can be threaded through the leather tip of the Handy Stick to extend its reach and make it more effective.

When tied around the horse's neck in a variety of positions, the string serves as a valuable reference point to help the handler maintain a correct, effective position (figs. 4.5 A & B).

Duct Tape

A bit of duct tape strategically placed on your training tools can help take the guesswork out of correct cue positioning (fig. 4.6).

Also recommended:

Boots

Using protective leg boots on a horse will help minimize strains and soreness. Be sure to keep your horse's legs and boots clean.

Gloves

Flexible, breathable, leather gloves can help you hold the rope and reins more securely. Should the horse pull against you, gloves will also save your hands from rope burns or blisters.

Place a strip of duct tape around the rope to mark the length of the Handy Stick from the clip. The duct tape is a useful reference point in many exercises when maintaining a specific distance from the horse is important.

5

AN INTRODUCTION
TO GROUNDWORK

Ground Control Equals Confidence

Remember: you earn the horse's respect when you control his movements forward, backward, left and right. That is why groundwork exercises are so important.

A lot of horses can seem relatively quiet until you take them away from their home environment. Then, they often act like completely different horses. They don't really believe you have enough leadership ability to keep them safe when other things are arousing their natural inclination to run from danger. The more confidence your horse has in you, the more situations and experiences you will be able to expose him to without him panicking and endangering himself—or you. He will trust you to keep him safe.

Constant Maintenance

Once your horse begins to recognize you as the leader in the relationship, he will test you on a daily basis to see if you still deserve his respect. Of course, some horses will do this more than others.

This aspect of working with horses frustrates many people. They want to address the issue of respect once, be done with it, and move on. Horses do not reason that way, however. Maintaining your leadership requires constant maintenance. You only need to watch a herd of horses to see what I mean.

Every herd has a pecking order. On occasion, a horse tries to climb a notch or two in the hierarchy. This applies to everyone—right up through the ranks. The lead horse knows there is always an opponent who hopes to take the leadership role away from him.

If horses challenge each other on a daily basis, what makes you think your horse won't regularly test you? You must not take this personally. When your horse tests your leadership, he only wants to assure himself that you

Facing Page
Training is a balancing act…
(see p. 43)

5.1

As your groundwork improves, so will your leadership skills.

deserve the position. You constantly need to prove to him that you are worth following. The good news is, as the horse's training progresses, he will respect your leadership more, and his challenges will become less of an issue.

Establishing your leadership role begins on the ground. The more groundwork exercises you know, the more tools you have at your disposal. The more tools you have, the more prepared you are to fix maintenance problems as they arrive.

The Importance of Groundwork

Groundwork involves more than leading your horse from the barn to the pasture. It is a step-by-step system designed to give you more control over your horse's movements .

I use a rope halter and a 14-foot lead line for most of my groundwork. I begin with simple exercises, such as getting the horse to flex and bend his neck. I move the horse out of my personal space. I also teach him to move specific parts of his body in response to simple cues.

This book contains a whole series of exercises that you can do with just a halter, a lead rope, and a Handy Stick. These very simple tools can help you move your horse forward, backward, left and right. Mastering these movements on the ground is essential before you ride.

5.2

As I move the horse forward, backward, left and right, I reinforce my role as leader.

Groundwork is the key to safely teaching your horse how to start, steer, and stop. It increases your chances of a successful ride.

Gordon McKinlay, one of the first horse trainers I ever worked for, told me, "The more times you are dumped on your head, the better your groundwork will get." Every time I got bucked off a horse, it was because I didn't do a good job preparing that horse for riding. I skipped my homework, and I paid the price. Every time I spat dirt out of my mouth, I knew exactly where I had cheated. We all want to cheat—until it catches up to us.

People often don't realize how important groundwork is until they have been injured. As their horse bucks them off, and they fly through the air, they think, "Should have done more groundwork…"

Groundwork is so important. In my opinion, you never get to a point where you no longer have to do it.

Sensitizing and Desensitizing

There are two categories in horse training. You either *sensitize* the horse to pressure, or you *desensitize* him. You can never do a combination of the two.

Anything that moves or creates motion has energy coming off of it. I call that energy "pressure."

In the same way that changing your car's oil keeps it running right, groundwork is an important part of your horse's maintenance program.

When *sensitizing*, you want the horse to *move away from pressure*. Some examples include:

• Pulling on the lead rope to bring the horse toward you.

• Holding your hands up to drive the horse out of your space and tell him to move away from you.

• Applying pressure with your legs when riding to signal the horse to move forward.

When sensitizing your horse, maintain the pressure until the horse either yields or moves. As soon as he responds, take the pressure away immediately and reward him.

Desensitizing, on the other hand, involves getting your horse to *stand still, relax,* or *not move to pressure*. Desensitizing is important if your horse is to:

• Stand calmly when being saddled.

• Not react when a rider waves his arms or swings a rope.

• Not spook at flapping flags, plastic bags, lawn ornaments, or horse show ribbons.

• Calmly accept the presence of traffic, dogs, or other horses.

To desensitize your horse, apply consistent, rhythmic pressure, until he relaxes and what you are doing no longer bothers him.

I Got Rhythm

When sensitizing or desensitizing, you must understand the need for *rhythm*.

Rhythm is an essential part of a horse's make-up. Every gait has rhythm. Even if the horse is standing still in the pasture, swatting flies, his tail will move with rhythm.

If you want a horse to move away from pressure, establish a rhythm with your cues. Maintain the rhythm until the horse responds. While keeping the rhythm steady, gradually increase the pressure to get the response you want.

Rhythm is *not* jerking on the horse's lead rope or reins. It is *not* inflicting a sharp and sudden pain. Rhythm does *not* speed up if you get angry.

If you establish a rhythm when sensitizing the horse, and gradually build in pressure until the horse responds, he will soon learn that if he doesn't listen to the early, easy cues, he can bank on stronger ones in the near future. Regular rhythm and increasing intensity will help your horse quickly become more responsive.

Keeping the System Balanced

As you have seen, when working with horses, you are either sensitizing them to pressure (getting them to soften, yield, and give), or desensitizing them (teaching them to relax, stand still, and trust you).

If you only sensitize, the horse will move, but he will become jumpy. If you only desensitize, the horse will soon be heavy, dull, and resistant. You don't want the horse nervous. And you don't want him asleep.

In general, every time you sensitize a horse and get him to move, you should balance the lesson with a desensitizing exercise. Here's why:

5.4

Training is a balancing act between sensitizing and desensitizing.

If you have a horse that is too desensitized, nothing will scare him—which is good. The downside is, he will also be unresponsive to your cues. He will either stand rooted to the spot when you want to go somewhere, or he will push and crowd into you.

If a horse is too sensitized, he will never relax and stand still. The good news is, at least your horse has forward motion. But an over-sensitized horse can be like a Ferrari with the accelerator stuck to the floor.

Quality Over Quantity

Many people want to get on their horses and ride. They say they have obligations to work and family and don't want to "waste time" on groundwork. Because your time is

valuable, you should use every minute with your horse to your advantage.

Let's say that because of your schedule, you can only ride three days a week. Many people will try to ride every other day. Instead, I strongly recommend that you try to ride several days in a row. Here's why:

When you go to ride on Monday, your horse has had Saturday and Sunday off. He is probably not interested in paying attention. (Many of us are like that on Mondays.) It doesn't matter whether you do groundwork, whether you ride, or do a bit of both—by the time you finish with your horse on Monday,

he should be listening and paying attention to you.

We'll assume you don't work with the horse again until Wednesday. Since he has had a day off, he probably doesn't listen very well, at first. By the time you finish working him on Wednesday, you may have his attention, but you probably won't have made any more progress than you did on Monday.

If you give the horse a few days off and don't ride him until Saturday, the same thing happens. Because he is fresh, listening to you is not his first priority. Again, you spend your time getting him focused and teaching the same lesson.

Though you have worked your horse three times during the week, you really haven't made much progress from session to session. If you can only ride your horse three days a week, I recommend that you do it three days in succession.

For example, ride your horse on Friday. Get him listening to you. On Saturday, the horse should start out with a good mental attitude. He should pay more attention than he did Friday. By the time you finish on Saturday, you have improved on Friday's lesson. When you start on Sunday, you should start right where you left off on Saturday and make even more improvement than you did the day before.

Even if you give your horse a vacation from Monday to Thursday, when you start again the following Friday, the progress has already been made.

Consistency Is Key

The key to all training techniques is *consistency*. Regularly working your horse gives him a chance to understand what you are teaching.

In the beginning, the horse may go through a bit of confusion about what you want from him. This is a normal part of the learning process.

As long as you are consistent, horses usually work things out very quickly. Soon, your horse will pick up on your body language. He will learn the cues that tell him whether you want him sensitized or desensitized. But he will never progress until you are absolutely clear, confident, and consistent (figs. 5.6 A–C).

A Byproduct of You

The level of respect your horse gives you, and the amount of progress he makes in his

5.6 A–C
Clear cues and consistent training allow you to work through the horse's initial resistance… and encourage him to try new things. Soon, he is ready to face new challenges.

training, are directly related to the time and effort you give him.

If you send a child to school five days a week and he fails, you have a reason to be upset. But if you only send that child to school once a week, you have no right to expect him to succeed because you haven't given him the tools or the knowledge to do so.

Horses are no different. We have to be willing to put the effort in first. Your horse is a byproduct of you. You can make progress if you only work your horse once or twice a week, but don't be disappointed at how long the training process takes. And don't expect your horse to be the most perfect, well-trained animal in the world if you are not prepared to give him the tools he needs to succeed.

Time and training result in a trusting, willing partner.

An Introduction to Groundwork 47

ESSENTIAL GROUNDWORK EXERCISES

The Hula Hoop

Tools Needed

Rope halter

14-foot lead rope

Handy Stick

Goal

To have the horse stand quietly, out of your immediate, personal space, giving you his undivided attention and looking at you with both eyes.

Why Do It?

As a trainer, you need your horse's respect and attention. Establishing your personal space aids your horse's learning and your safety.

Consider the weight difference. Your horse is roughly ten times your weight. A horse may not necessarily mean to hurt you, but because of his body mass, if he comes into contact with you, it can hurt.

Most injuries from disrespectful horses, including kicking, biting, and running over people, occur because the horse is too close to his handler. Your horse should be close only if you specifically invite him to come near you. Otherwise, he should keep a respectful, safe distance.

Teaching Steps

1. Establish your *Hula Hoop* space. Draw an imaginary circle on the ground around you with the Handy Stick. Stand in the center of the circle (fig. 6.1).
2. Hold the lead rope with enough slack so that the horse can stand outside your Hula Hoop without putting any pressure on the rope. If you can touch any part of the horse—even his nose—with your stick, he is too close.
3. Use your Handy Stick in the *handshake hold*. Rhythmically tap the Handy Stick on

Facing Page

Yielding the Forequarters *teaches the horse to move forward and around while respecting your space (see p. 77).*

The area inside your Hula Hoop is your personal space.

Master this exercise before attempting any other training. It is the first step toward earning your horse's respect and focusing his attention on you.

whatever part of the horse you can reach—whatever is in your circle. Gradually increase the pressure of your tapping until you get the response you want and the horse moves backward.

4. Once the horse is out of your Hula Hoop, bump or jerk the lead rope with rhythm until you get "two eyes" on you. When the horse looks directly at you, stop.

5. Every time your horse takes his eyes off you, bump the lead rope until he focuses on you again.

Common Handler Mistakes

• Being ineffective. Most people want to tap the horse only once or twice. Continue tapping and increase the pressure until the horse moves out of your space.

• Following the horse. When the horse starts moving in response to your taps, keep your feet still. Stay inside your Hula Hoop.

Common Horse Mistakes

• Creeping in close to you. Tap with the Handy Stick to get the horse out of your space and keep him out of it. Tap the lead rope, or whatever body part you can reach, to discourage the horse from creeping in close to you.

Troubleshooting

• If you can touch any part of the horse with your Handy Stick, continue tapping. Moving out of your Hula Hoop is the only way the horse can avoid being tapped.

Tips for Success

• Tap with rhythm. Count out loud to keep your rhythm. 1-2-3-4. 1-2-3-4! **1-2-3-4!**

• Each new set of numbers increases the energy of your tapping. Start with low energy. Move to medium. Go to high, if necessary. Don't nag at your horse with half-hearted taps. Be effective.

Desensitizing Exercises

The purpose of *Desensitizing Exercises* is to show the horse that though we want his respect, he has nothing to fear from us.

In Australia, where men make a living traveling from station to station breaking colts, desensitizing horses to a variety of stimuli is a vital part of making them fit for work.

Australian horse breakers want to make sure that moving a saddle and saddle bag, or cracking a stock whip all around the horse does not terrify the animal. If you can desensitize the horse to such things from the ground, he is less likely to be frightened of them when you are riding.

Desensitizing to the Rope

6.2
Desensitizing to the Rope takes rhythm and patience.

Tools Needed
Rope halter
14-foot lead rope

Goal
To be able to throw the lead rope over and around any part of the horse's body while he stands relaxed.

Why Do It?

This begins the important process of making sure the horse doesn't fear us or our tools. It helps him tell the difference between your cues for moving and standing still.

Desensitizing the horse to a rope also teaches him not to panic when he feels a rope around his neck or legs. This exercise could help save him from serious injury if he ever becomes entangled in a piece of equipment.

Teaching Steps

1. Stand at a 45-degree angle to the horse's shoulder, facing his withers. Hold the lead rope with the hand closest to the horse, about two feet from the snap. Hold the end of the rope in your other hand, leaving a "tail" about two or three feet long.

2. Gently throw the rope tail over the horse's back. Drag it back toward the ground.

Repeat with repetitive rhythm until the rope can land anywhere on the horse's topline—from his withers to his haunches. When the horse stands quietly, repeat the exercise on the other side.

3. Lengthen the tail to approximately five feet. Repeat the exercise.

4. Repeat the exercise, throwing the entire rope over the horse's back.

5. When the horse is comfortable with the whole rope being pitched over his back, desensitize his entire body. Do the topline first: withers and back, hindquarters and neck. Then do the hind legs and forelegs (fig. 6.3).

Common Handler Mistakes

• Pulling on the lead shank with one hand when dragging the rope back with the other. To avoid jerking on the horse's head, put your thumb in your pocket, or raise your hand toward the horse's head like a traffic cop.

- Having too much slack in the lead rope. Have just enough slack in the rope so you do not pull on the halter. Too much slack could allow the horse to turn away from you in avoidance.

- Backing away from a pushy horse. Keep your feet still. Retreating invites the horse to push over you even more. If necessary, reestablish your *Hula Hoop* space (p. 49) before continuing this exercise.

- Not keeping both of the horse's eyes on you. Every time the horse doesn't want to look at you, bump on the lead rope, and bring his head back toward you.

- Throwing too much rope, too soon. Start small. Throw a longer rope tail as the horse relaxes.

- Loss of repetitive motion. Have rhythm with your arm and the rope no matter what happens. If the horse moves around, or if the rope gets tangled, don't stop moving your arm. The longer the pause between each throw, the more the horse will think he is responding correctly.

- Stopping when the horse reacts. If the horse moves or jumps, and you take the stimulus away, this teaches him that he did the right thing. Keep gently, rhythmically swinging the rope at whatever spot makes the horse twitch until he relaxes.

- Not using approach and retreat. Apply pressure and don't retreat until the horse stands still and relaxes.

Common Horse Problems

- Running around in circles. Don't try to stop the horse. Stay in position beside his shoulder. Bump the lead shank with rhythm to encourage him to continue looking at you. Continue throwing the rope with rhythm. The horse should soon stand still and relax.

- Trying to run into you. Keep the hand holding the lead shank up near the horse's face. If he starts pushing on you, pump the air with your hand—warning him to keep away. If necessary, bump his jaw out of your space.

- Backing away. Don't try to stop the horse. Keep throwing the rope with rhythm until he stops on his own and relaxes.

- Kicking out. Stay in position beside the shoulder so you don't get kicked. Continue the exercise until the horse stands still and relaxes.

Troubleshooting

- When throwing the entire rope over the horse's back, fling it as far behind you as possible when you pull it to the ground. This will put it in position for easier throwing. Throw the rope over your horse as if you were pitching a softball to someone on the opposite side. Let the rope fly completely out of your hand.

Tips for Success

- To make it easier to throw the rope over the horse's neck, stand at the horse's shoulder, facing his head.

- Think in terms of snakes. The two-foot tail is a garden snake. The 5-foot tail is a rattlesnake. The whole rope is a python.

✳ *Cecelia*

"You have to get the rope out behind you in order to throw it without getting tangled. What really helped me was when Clinton got on the other side of the horse and had me

6.4

"Holding my left hand up like a traffic cop helped keep me from pulling on Smacks' head. It kept me more aware of that hand."

throw the rope to him as if I were throwing a ball. When I got the hang of it, I could fling it over every time."

※ *Paula*

"Lengthening the rope and throwing it over the horse was harder for me. It was easi-est when the rope was shorter. But Clinton emphasized keeping the throwing rhythm, even if the rope got tangled around my arm.

"Fancy handled this well; she is fairly laid back. But I have a really 'goosey' horse at home that this will be great for."

Desensitizing to the Handy Stick and String

6.5

Desensitizing to the Handy Stick and String teaches the horse to relax around your training tools.

Tools Needed
Rope halter
14-foot lead rope
Handy Stick with string attached

Goal
To throw, slap, and swing the Handy Stick and string all over the horse, including the air space around him while he stands quiet and relaxed.

Why Do It?
Desensitizing the horse to an object that moves and makes noise teaches him that he doesn't need to fear such things. It also teaches the horse to pay attention to his handler's body language.

Stage One—Rubbing

Teaching Steps
1. Stand at a 45-degree angle to the horse's shoulder, facing the horse's rear. Hold the lead rope with the hand closest to the horse, about two feet from the snap. Hold the Handy Stick in your other hand.
2. Begin at the topline. Rub all along the horse's withers and back, hindquarters and neck in a repetitive, rhythmic way.
3. In the same manner, rub the hind legs, forelegs, and under the belly, in that order. Desensitize one side of the horse. Repeat the exercise, in the same order, on the other side (fig. 6.6).

Common Handler Mistakes

• Losing the repetitive movement. Count out loud or keep time to a song in order to help you maintain your rhythm.

• Stopping when the horse moves or reacts. Taking the stimulus away from the horse only serves to reward him for moving. Instead, continue doing exactly what caused the horse to react, until he stands quietly.

• Trying to make the horse stop moving. Let the horse move. Keep his eyes on you until he wants to stop. Let stopping be his choice.

Stage Two—String Toss

Teaching Steps

1. Hold the horse as in Step 1 of *Stage One*.

2. Swing the Handy Stick and string over the horse. The tip of the Handy Stick should land softly on the horse's back, allowing the string to fall on the other side.

3. Draw the Handy Stick toward the ground so the string slides off the horse's back. Repeat with rhythm until the horse stands still. Stop. Rub him. Begin again.

4. When the horse is comfortable with the topline, desensitize the hindquarters, hind legs, and forelegs (fig. 6.7).

Common Handler Mistakes

• Allowing the horse to take both eyes off you. If the horse walks around, bump on the lead rope so he continues facing you.

• Holding the lead shank too short. Give

You should be able to toss the string anywhere on your horse without him moving or flinching.

your horse about two feet of lead. Make him responsible for standing still, rather than trying to physically hold him in place.

• Holding the lead shank too long. More than two feet of lead could allow your horse to spin around enough to kick you. Be safety conscious.

Stage Three—Slapping the Ground

Teaching Steps

1. Hold the horse as in Step 1 of *Stage One*.
2. Hold your Handy Stick as far away from the horse as possible. Rotate your arm in a circular motion and rhythmically slap the ground with medium energy.
3. Have the horse keep both eyes on you.

Keep slapping the ground with rhythm.

4. When your horse stands calmly, move the Handy Stick closer until he thinks about moving. Stay there, slapping with rhythm, until the horse relaxes.
5. Stop. Rub him with the Handy Stick. Repeat the exercise on the same side, moving the Handy Stick closer each time.
6. When the horse is desensitized on one side, repeat Steps 1 through 5 on the other side.
7. Stand about 10 feet in front of your horse. Gently slap the Handy Stick and string from side-to-side. When your horse relaxes, stop, and rub his face. Repeat.
8. Every day, increase the amount of force you use to slap the ground. Your goal is to whack the ground, *hard*, in a 360-degree

6.8

Swing the Handy Stick with your whole arm. Use large, circular motions.

circle all around your horse, while he stands quiet and relaxed.

Common Handler Mistakes

• Starting too close to the horse. Stretch the Handy Stick out as far as your arm can reach to establish a starting point.

• Starting with too much intensity. Begin slapping the ground with mild energy. Increase the intensity when your horse is calm and quiet.

• Stopping the rhythmic slapping when the horse thinks about moving. If your horse is on the verge of moving, stay where you are—keep doing what you are doing—until he stands still and relaxes. *Then* stop and rub him.

Common Horse Problems

• Running in circles. Bump repeatedly on the lead shank. Make it uncomfortable for him to run around and not look at you.

• Running backward. As long as the horse has two eyes on you, let him back up. Stay with him. Continue the exercise until your horse consistently stands still and relaxes. Then stop and rub him.

• Kicking out or rearing. Stay a safe distance from the horse. Continue the exercise in a gentle, repetitive manner. Ignore the bad behavior, if possible. The horse will learn that these behaviors will not eliminate the pressure.

Troubleshooting

• If your horse is very sensitive and easily frightened, find a starting point. You may want to put your back to a fence to discourage him from running around you. You may want to do the exercise in a round pen. Use less intensity if you must, but *do not stop until the horse stands still and relaxes.*

Tips for Success

• Just because your horse is confident on one side doesn't mean he will be on the other. When you switch sides, start from the beginning and gradually build intensity again.

• Desensitize at the beginning of every lesson, every day. Also, practice one or more desensitizing exercises after every sensitizing lesson.

❋ *Cecelia*

"For a hunter that goes on actual foxhunts with dogs and whips, this is a critical exercise. I couldn't believe how quickly Smacks grew accustomed to the rhythmical whacking around him.

"Be aware of lash placement. When you are smacking the ground *hard*, you will feel awful if you misjudge and hit the horse."

❋ *Paula*

"I am shorter, so it was hard for me to hold onto the handle of the Handy Stick and do all that swinging. After a while, I learned to let the weight of the Handy Stick just pull my arm around in the circle.

"A couple of times, Fancy reacted more than I thought she would to a new desensitizing exercise. It is so important to do something easy that the horse already knows before upping the pressure and desensitizing her to something new."

Disengage the Hindquarters

Disengaging the Hindquarters teaches the horse to move his hind end away from pressure.

Tools Needed

Rope halter
14-foot lead rope
Handy Stick
String used as a drive line (see p. 35)

Goal

To *Disengage the Hindquarters* any time you apply pressure toward them, stopping the horse's forward momentum.

Why Do It?

When an Australian colt-breaker saddles a young, "broncy" colt for the first time, he knows the horse's hindquarters are his gas pedal. He wants to be able to move the hindquarters if the horse tries to buck with the saddle or kicks out.

If you can control the hindquarters, you will have much better control of your horse's body and his forward motion. Using your body language to yield the horse's hindquarters is useful when trying to catch the horse in the stall or the pasture. Furthermore, teaching the horse to disengage his hindquarters on the ground sets the stage for him to readily yield his hindquarters when asked under saddle.

Stage One—Yield the Hindquarters

Teaching Steps

Before beginning this exercise, always rub the horse on his hindquarters with the Handy Stick.

1. Hold the lead rope with the hand closest to the horse, about two feet from the snap. With the other hand, use the Handy Stick in the *handshake hold.*
2. Stand slightly behind the drive line, facing the horse's rear. Raise the arm holding the lead rope to block the front end from moving forward into you.
3. Crouch forward slightly and look at the horse's hindquarters. If the horse doesn't move, tap the air above his hip with small, rhythmic taps.
4. If the horse still doesn't move, use the same repetitive motion to tap lightly just behind his hip. (See figs. 6.10 A & B.)
5. When the horse takes one correct step, stop tapping. Rub the hip until the horse stops moving.
6. When the horse consistently takes one correct step, ask for two steps, then three, and so on. Remember to rub him to a stop at the end of each try.

Common Handler Mistakes

- Beginning too aggressively. **Start gently. Increase the pressure as needed, but always give the horse a chance to get it right.**
- Getting in front of the drive line. **Refer to the string on your horse's neck to maintain the correct position.**
- Not rubbing the horse to a stop. **Rubbing helps the horse learn to read the changes in your body language. Rubbing also serves to desensitize the horse so he doesn't become jumpy when he sees the Handy Stick.**
- Not letting the horse rest between tries. **Let the horse learn that when he does the right thing, he gets a reward.**
- Cueing without rhythm. **Count out loud to help you maintain your rhythm.**
- Dropping the arm holding the lead rope. **Raise your hand up to block the horse's front end and keep him from running forward or pushing into you.**
- Releasing the pressure before the horse moves correctly. **Watch your horse's inside hind leg. Don't stop the pressure and rub him until he steps across and in front of the outside hind leg.**

Common Horse Problems

- Running forward. **Keep your hand high to block the horse's forward motion. If you must, bump on the lead rope in the direction of his withers to keep him from charging forward.**
- Backing up. **Follow the horse. Make sure you stay behind the drive line. Patiently apply pressure. Wait for him to find the answer. Keep tapping with rhythm until he disengages correctly.**
- Kicking out at you. **Smack him on the butt *hard*, one time. This often surprises the horse so much that he doesn't try kicking out again. Every time the horse kicks, whack him, once, with the Handy Stick. Be black or white. Continue as if the incident never happened.**
- Biting at you. **Keep your lead rope hand high. If the horse snaps at you, bump his jaw away with your elbow.**
- Rearing. **A horse can't rear if his hindquarters are disengaging. Stay a safe distance**

6.10 A & B

To yield the hindquarters correctly, cue until… the horse places the inside hind leg across and in front of the outside hind leg.

away, but tap the hindquarters until he steps across. Then, rub him.

✳ *Cecelia*

"I forgot that I was to tap the air first. Smacks is very sensitive. When I was consistent about tapping the air to begin the cue, I hardly needed to touch him half of the time.

"Cueing for the disengage uses several motor skills at one time. It is definitely a learning process just getting your body used to making the motions effectively. I would try to use one hand to cue the hindquarters to move and forget to keep my other hand up beside his eye to keep his head away from me. It's like a ballet. I am asking the horse to dance, but I need to learn the steps myself.

"I like using the string around the horse's neck as a reference point. It makes it much easier to stay in the correct position.

"It is so important to be sure your body language is clear. Open up, relax, and stand calm to draw the horse to you. Crouch down and close in on yourself to drive him away.

"The importance of doing these exercises in sequence was made clear early in our training. We had established our *Hula Hoop* space and done some desensitizing work before beginning this exercise. On the very first day, when the other horse was misbehaving, my horse's reaction was superb. He relocated his body to get out of her way, but he didn't jump on me. He respected my space. And, he didn't wig out. Believe me when I say how unusual that was for him! I saw a difference in his attitude immediately."

✳ *Paula*

"What helped me most was Clinton telling me to focus only on Fancy's feet. You have to watch the feet. As soon as the hind leg closest to you crosses in front of the other, stop the cue and rub the horse. That is the correct response. That is what you are waiting to reward. Nothing else really matters.

"The concept of body language is consistent with all the techniques Clinton has shown us so far. The more we do it, the more we get used to doing it. Soon, putting your hand up to create a 'wall' in front of the horse's head—to keep her from stepping on you or running her shoulder into you—becomes habit.

"So many people will back off of a cue when they should do just the opposite and stick with it. I am as guilty of that as the next person. I liked having Clinton telling me, 'Stay with her... stay with her...' until we made progress."

Stage Two—Disengage and Turn to Face You

Teaching Steps

1. Follow Steps 1 through 4 of *Stage One*.
2. When the horse begins to disengage his hindquarters, tap with more energy (fig. 6.11).
3. Tap until the horse swings his hindquarters away from you and turns to face you with both eyes. Rub him for facing you. Rub his hindquarters before beginning the exercise again.
4. Teach the exercise to both sides.

Common Handler Mistakes

• Not stopping in time. When the horse's head points in your direction, rub him and reward him for giving you his attention.

• Pulling the horse's head toward you.

6.11
*Encourage the horse
to disengage his
hindquarters with
energy.*

Use the lead rope only to reinforce the cue. The horse should drive his hindquarters away in order to disengage.

- Running after the hindquarters. If you run, the horse will never be able to turn fast enough to face you. Walk forward at a steady pace. Don't walk faster than you are tapping.
- Walking too closely to the horse. Walk in a wide arc toward the horse's hindquarters. Give the horse enough room to bring his head and neck around and face you.

Common Horse Problems

- Anticipation. If the horse wants to move his hindquarters before you ask him to, make sure that you rub him to a stop. Also, make sure that you aren't tapping too aggressively. Try rubbing and then retreating with the Handy Stick several times between each disengage. If the horse insists on moving, make him move with energy for 10 to 15 circles. When you think he wants to stop, rub him.
- Yielding lazily. Get more aggressive with your tapping. Don't nag. Tap with high energy until the horse takes you seriously and moves his feet *now*.

Troubleshooting

- If the horse kicks at you, be sure you aren't nagging at him with your cues. Taps that don't stop and don't accomplish anything will often frustrate the horse and cause him to kick out. Also, make sure that you aren't tapping too hard. Start out with a light tap in the air over the hip. Then slowly increase the pressure.

Tips for Success

- Practice Disengaging the Hindquarters in your daily routine. Get the horse to turn and face you while leading him to the pasture. Ask him to yield a step or two before feeding him in his stall or while you are grooming him. The better you can perform this exercise on the ground, the better "brake" you will have under saddle.

❋ *Cecelia*

"Smacks doesn't wheel around like a Quarter Horse. I didn't immediately take that into consideration. I wanted to see a Quarter Horse spin, so I kept walking aggressively and giving him the disengage cue. I was essentially chasing him. Clinton reminded me to remember to stop and reward the effort my horse was making.

"I had a tendency to kind of sneak around him. I had to learn to get in position faster and get the job done.

"I really like *Stage Two*. It sure gets the horse's attention quickly."

❋ *Paula*

"I had to remember to stop and reward her. Once Fancy understood what I wanted and yielded several steps at once, I wanted to keep practicing. I must have done about twenty circles! But I need to remember to reward the try.

"I also need to remember not to nag. If she ignores light tapping, now that she knows what is expected of her, I need to increase the pressure to be effective, rather than just keep tapping her."

Backing

A willing horse backs straight away from you with energy.

Tools Needed

Rope halter

14-foot lead rope with duct tape

Handy Stick

Goal

To cause the horse to energetically back away from you, reacting to your body language.

Why Do It?

Backing helps reinforce the importance of a personal *Hula Hoop* space and encourages the horse to read your body language. It also sets the stage for establishing a non-aggressive means of discipline.

While growing up in Australia, I encountered hundreds of situations where I needed to be able to back my horse from the ground.

Backing away from pressure is important in order to unload a horse from a truck or trailer. Sometimes, when working in confined areas, backing is the only safe way out of a situation.

Some methods of backing lend themselves to certain situations better than others.

• *Tap the Air* teaches the horse to respond to your body language—even if you are standing still.

• *Wiggle, Wave, Walk, and Whack* and *Marching* reinforce the concept of your personal space. The horse learns to get out of your way, rather than expecting you to get out of his.

• *Disengage and Back* teaches the horse to back up, even when you are not in front of him. This prepares him to respond better in crowded situations, such as unloading from a trailer.

Tap the Air

Teaching Steps

1. Stand about two feet in front of your horse, facing him. Hold the lead rope at the duct tape. Allow plenty of slack in the rope. With your other hand, use the Handy Stick in the *handshake hold*.

2. With the Handy Stick, tap the air in front of your horse's face with short up-and-down strokes. Tap four times.

3. Increase the pressure every four taps until you are effective. Tap the rope; tap the rope harder; tap the clip on the rope; then firmly tap the horse's nose, if necessary. Tap with rhythm, increasing the intensity of your pressure until the horse backs up two steps.

4. Any time the horse takes two steps back, stop cueing. Rub him gently on the face, between the eyes, with the end of the Handy Stick.

5. When your horse backs two steps consistently, ask for four steps. Over time, gradually ask for more steps, and use less energy for the cue.

6.13

*When you **Tap the Air**, hold the Handy Stick up so the horse can see it from the moment you begin cueing. Keep it over the rope and tap downward.*

Common Handler Mistakes

• Tapping the air too aggressively. Start out with soft cues. Build in intensity only if the horse doesn't respond.

• Too much time between stages. If the horse doesn't respond after a set of four taps, immediately increase the pressure. There should be no lag time between counting to four and beginning again at one.

• Not regulating the pressure correctly. Every new set of four taps brings a slight increase in intensity. Don't jump from low to high energy. Build gradually, always looking for the chance to stop and reward the horse for trying.

• Nagging. If you tap and tap, and the horse doesn't back up, you are teaching him to ignore you. Be effective.

• Asking for too much at first. Take the pressure away from the horse after only two steps back. This rewards him and lets him know he has given you the desired response. If you insist on the horse backing up several steps too soon, he won't learn that backing up makes the pressure stop. Eventually, he will become desensitized to your cues and ignore you.

• Holding the lead rope too long or too short. Hold the duct tape. It will help keep you in a good position for cueing.

• Letting the lead rope tighten as the horse backs. The horse should never run into pressure from the halter when he is backing. Drift with him—even if he backs long after you have stopped cueing. Rub him on the face with the Handy Stick until he stops.

• Tapping beside the nose. This will cause the horse to turn sideways, away from you. Tap the air in front of his nose. Keep both of his eyes on you.

Common Horse Problems

• Trying to run over you. Stand your ground and rap him on the nose with your Handy Stick. Make it uncomfortable for him to run into you. Make him move out of your space—not the other way around. Be as firm as necessary to get the job done.

• Throwing his head up in the air when backing. In the beginning, this is normal. Once the horse's feet unlock and start moving with energy, the head will come down.

• Rearing or striking out with the front feet. If necessary, get a bit further away from the horse, but apply the same rhythmic pressure. If the horse is reacting out of fear, take a bit of the pressure off, but don't stop cueing. The instant the horse takes a step backward, rub him, and reward him. Try to act as if it's not happening. A horse can't rear forever. Let him realize there is no reward for rearing— only backing.

Troubleshooting

• Concentrate on gradually increasing the intensity of your cues. Be ready to immediately stop the pressure and reward the slightest try.

Tips for Success

• Don't ask for too many steps in a row for the first few sessions. Instead, do many repetitions of asking for only two or four steps. As the horse progresses, ask for more. When your horse can do that well, proceed to *Wiggle, Wave, Walk and Whack.*

❋ *Cecelia*

"When I ask for the backup, I know to stop the cue when the horse begins respond-

Wave the Handy Stick vigorously in a wide path from side-to-side in front of you.

ing. But stopping the cue doesn't mean stopping my feet. Clinton reminded me to drift forward while Smacks was backing and rub him until he stopped."

✳ *Paula*

"My Handy Stick kept getting wrapped up because I was hitting the rope with the middle of the stick. Tapping the rope with the end of the stick made things easier.

"Fancy hasn't backed up much in her life. When she walks forward, she has learned that I will back out of her way. All that has changed, but it took a bit to convince her that I meant what I said.

"After a few days, when Fancy was backing well, the medium energy cues fell away. It was either tap the air or whack with energy. Soon, all I had to do was tap the air and Fancy would back up *now*."

Wiggle, Wave, Walk, and Whack

Teaching Steps

1. Stand as for Step 1 of *Tap the Air*. Wiggle the wrist of the hand holding the rope back-and-forth for four counts.

2. If you get no response, use your whole arm to move the rope horizontally with more energy. At the same time, wave the Handy Stick back-and-forth underneath the rope (fig. 6.14). Crisscross your arms. Walk toward your horse.

3. If the horse doesn't back, let the Handy Stick run into him. Maintain the same rhythm and motions with your arms. Be effective.

4. As soon as the horse backs two steps out of your space, stop. Rub him on his chest with the Handy Stick. Repeat. When the horse consistently takes two steps back with energy, ask for a few more steps.

Common Handler Mistakes

- Pulling the horse to a stop. When you want to stop, take the pressure away. Drift with your horse until he stops backing.
- Not touching the horse with the Handy Stick. If you don't follow through when you ask the horse to do something, he will never take you seriously. Swing the Handy Stick with energy. Let the horse decide to back away from it.
- Being ineffective. If the horse isn't moving, swing the Handy Stick harder. Get the job done.
- Asking for too many steps at first. Concentrate on getting two good steps, then stop applying pressure and rub the horse.
- Not letting the horse rest. Always rub the horse to a stop and let him think a bit before cueing him to back up again.
- Removing pressure when the horse's feet slow. Quit applying pressure when the horse is moving with energy. Don't allow him to determine how much effort to put into the exercise.

Common Horse Problems

- Jumping off to one side. Don't run out in front of the horse to correct him. Bump his nose back in line with you and continue. Maintain walking in a straight line.
- Trying to run over you or refusing to back. If the horse refuses to move out of your space, tap him underneath the jaw with the Handy Stick. Make it worth his while to get out of your way.

Troubleshooting

- If your horse does not respond the way you want with this exercise, work on Tap the Air again.
- Many horses will back up slowly. Insist on a "Yes I can!" attitude. Have high expectations for you and your horse.

Tips for Success

- One or two firm, high-energy taps with the Handy Stick is better than a thousand little nags. This ultimately teaches the horse to respond to the slightest signal you give, rather than dulling his senses by repeated ineffective tapping. Don't be a "nagging mother."

❊ *Cecelia*

"The Wiggle, Wag way was easy for us, because Smacks was already in backing mode after working on Tap the Air.

"Smacks pays a lot of attention to body language. After a short while, it only took the slightest bit of wiggle to get Smacks to reverse. Many times, my body language of stepping forward was enough for him.

"I had to concentrate on making my cues clear and not nagging. Clinton says the 'wimpy wiggle' just makes the horse ignore you. That isn't the goal at all.

"I was thrilled to have Smacks' attention the whole time. Sometimes, we weren't working while Clinton and Paula focused on Fancy. Smacks knew he could clock out, but when I needed him, he was ready."

❊ *Paula*

"When we started learning this way of backing, Fancy didn't even think of moving out of my space. I had to learn that if the horse doesn't get out of your way, you have to be much more assertive in order to be effective and get a response.

"Clinton is not even remotely kidding about increasing the pressure. Fancy had plenty of opportunities to respond to gentle cues. But if the horse doesn't respond to a cue in the air, tap the horse. If the tap doesn't get a response, increase the pressure.

"Clinton took over for a while because I was too wimpy to increase the pressure to be effective. He had to tap under her jaw and chin—fairly forcefully at first—in order to get any response from her at all!

"It took a lot to convince Fancy that I was serious. But it was necessary. I can see how dangerous it is to let your horse ignore you in anything. It ends up making her ignore you more and more until you are afraid or frustrated and she knows it.

"If I had been at home, without Clinton there to show me how to increase the pressure until she responded, I would have probably gone back to a ground exercise that I knew she would do, like Tap the Air. I am sure there will be other times in her training when I am not being effective. So I will just go back to something where I *am* effective. Then we'll try again.

"It took some doing, but the difference in her attitude toward me is amazing. There is no fear at all; there is respect, and that is something new."

Marching

Teaching Steps

1. Stand in front of your horse. Hold the lead shank in your left hand halfway between the duct tape and the clip. With your right hand, hold the Handy Stick in the *ski pole hold* (fig. 6.15).
2. Raising your elbows and your knees, begin marching in place. After four counts, march

toward your horse. Swing the Handy Stick toward the horse's chest in time to your marching.

3. If the horse doesn't back up by the time you are close enough to touch him, let the Handy Stick tap him firmly on the chest. As soon as the horse backs up two steps, stop cueing. Rub him on the chest with the Handy Stick until he stands still.

4. Repeat. As the horse progresses, ask for more and more steps.

Common Handler Mistakes

• Not marching with exaggeration. Exaggerate your body language, especially at first.

• Not following through. Use your whole arm to swing the Handy Stick beside you. Use the momentum to bring the Handy Stick forward, tapping your horse firmly on the chest, if necessary.

• Holding the lead rope too long. Holding the lead rope halfway between the duct tape and the clip makes it easier to correct a horse that runs sideways to avoid you.

• Stopping too soon. Don't release the pressure until the horse gives you two steps backward.

• Forgetting to rub the horse between each exercise. Rub the horse on the chest between each set of cues to ensure that he doesn't get overly sensitive about being touched with the Handy Stick.

Common Horse Problems

• Running around in circles. Bump down sharply on the lead shank. Make it uncomfortable to ignore or avoid you.

• Trying to run over you. If tapping the horse sharply on the chest is not effective, tap him with rhythm underneath his jaw with the Handy Stick. Be effective.

• Backing crookedly. Bump on the lead rope to pull the horse's head in the direction of the hindquarters. You can also firmly tap the horse's neck or shoulder to make him back in a straight line.

• Jumping off to the side. Tug sharply down on the lead rope with rhythm as you march forward.

• Dragging his feet or being lazy. Tap aggressively under the horse's chest to encourage him to pick up his shoulders and lift his feet.

Troubleshooting

• If the horse doesn't respond to your cues, bump down on the lead rope as you march toward him. Remember to reward the slightest step backward.

Tips for Success

• Do not try to outrun your horse. Give him the opportunity to succeed.

✳ *Cecelia*

"Every new exercise builds on the ones before. Occasionally, when we concentrate on something new, I will get lax on some thing we have already covered—like allowing Smacks to invade my personal space. But now I am aware of how to quickly deal with the situation so we can get back to work.

"These exercises look deceptively easy. There is more physicality involved than meets the eye. I appreciated Clinton encouraging me to 'stay with it.' Just when you might think about quitting, it is so important to keep going until you get a response.

"I had to learn not to stop on a slow note.

If I stopped my cues when Smacks was slowly drifting backward, he would become less and less responsive. The time to stop my cues is when he is backing-up smartly, then drift with him to a stop. That way *I* decide when the backing stops."

✳ *Paula*

"I used to march in the band. At first, for this way of cueing, I stepped too high and didn't use my arms enough. Amazingly, Fancy responded—even when the cues weren't perfect!

"Fancy's biggest problem was moving forward or sideways instead of backing-up. Clinton reminded me that moving sideways isn't trying. It is avoidance. To correct her when she tried to turn, I would either pull the lead rope in the opposite direction or put the Handy Stick up and block her path. It took some doing to convince her that it was in her best interest to back up when I asked, instead of plowing forward into me.

"If the horse tries to avoid you, don't back off and regroup. Don't stop. Keep going. Keep cueing until you are effective and the horse tries to do what you are asking.

"I liked the fact that Clinton gave us permission to get aggressive with our horses. I tend to be a little timid. But the more I work with her, the more confident I get.

"In the beginning, Fancy was a little dull—she didn't want to back up with any enthusiasm. Now she knows I will keep increasing the pressure until she moves with some energy. The second day we worked on backing-up, the difference in her attitude amazed me. She was so responsive! I hardly had to increase the pressure of my cues at all."

Disengage and Back

Teaching Steps

1. Wrap the lead rope around the horse's neck to keep it out of the way. Stand at a 45-degree angle to the horse's shoulder, facing his rear.
2. With the hand nearest the horse, hold the lead rope at the snap (fig. 6.16). With the other hand, use the Handy Stick in the *handshake hold.*
3. *Disengage the Hindquarters* in a full circle, 360 degrees. After the horse has completed the circle, before his feet stop moving, jiggle the lead rope up and down, encouraging him to back up.
4. If the horse doesn't back with energy, bump the halter up-and-down on the horse's nose. You may also have to tap him on the chest, holding the Handy Stick in *ski pole hold* (figs. 6.17 A & B).
5. As soon as the horse backs up one or two steps, stop and rub him on the hindquarters with the Handy Stick.
6. Teach this exercise from both sides. Once the horse understands what is asked of him, yielding the hindquarters isn't necessary. Just stand beside him and jiggle the clip on the lead rope.

Common Handler Mistakes

• Letting the horse stop before backing. The whole reason for yielding the hindquarters is to get the feet moving. If the feet stop, yield the hindquarters again before asking the horse to back up.

• Pushing with the halter. Most horses will push against you if you push on them. Instead

*The horse must master **Disengage the Hindquarters** (p. 60) before being taught this exercise.*

*Hold the lead rope
like an ice cream
cone.*

of pushing, create some energy by jiggling, bumping, and tapping to drive the horse back.

• Nagging. Don't bump the horse with every step he takes. As soon as the feet move, stop cueing.

• Beginning too aggressively. Always start with a small jiggle. Give the horse a chance to respond before increasing the pressure to a bump or a tap.

Common Horse Problems

• Horse anticipates disengaging the hindquarters. If your horse starts moving his hindquarters before you have given him the cue, spend some time rubbing him and desensitizing him to the Handy Stick.

Many of the problems you may encounter are the same problems your horse presented in the previous backing exercises. The corrections are the same.

Disengaging the Hindquarters with energy...allows the horse's momentum to carry him backward.

Essential Groundwork Exercises 75

Troubleshooting

• If the horse tucks his head without moving his feet, continue applying pressure. Use the Handy Stick more aggressively until the horse backs.

Tips for Success

• Always quit on a good note. If your horse isn't responding the way you had hoped, reevaluate your starting point. End the session when the horse tries and is better than when you started.

✳ *Cecelia*

"I once yielded Smacks' hindquarters, then asked him to back right into the fence. I put him in a situation where he couldn't succeed. There is so much to be aware of.

"Horses catch on quickly. Clinton made a good point—don't drill and drill and drill until the horse becomes dull. Do a bit. When the horse seems to be catching on, even if you don't have the hang of all the physical motor skills yet, don't keep working the horse just so you get better. Stop. Do something else. Then go back and practice some more.

"I like how the groundwork is improving Smacks' attitude. After only two days, I saw a profound change in him."

✳ *Paula*

"The difference in Fancy after only two days was incredible. The horses react quickly— more quickly than you can think, sometimes.

"This exercise seemed relatively easy since Fancy had already learned to disengage her hindquarters. Every new thing builds on some earlier lesson. If you have done that lesson thoroughly, the new thing you teach isn't hard.

"Clinton had to tell me to stop! I wanted to keep going; at first I thought it was all about getting my horse to back up a lot. But it is more about getting her light and responsive. As soon as I see her feet lighten up and she moves with energy, I should stop cueing."

Yielding the Forequarters

6.18

Yielding the Forequarters helps give you control of the horse's front end.

Tools Needed

Rope halter

14-foot lead rope

Handy Stick

Goal

To drive the horse's front end away from you. To have the horse pivot around the hindquarters, crossing his front feet over each other.

Why Do It?

This exercise teaches the horse to move his front end out of your space. Control of the horse's front end equals control of the horse's direction. Your horse's respect will increase when he realizes that you have the ability to determine where he puts his feet.

Teaching Steps

1. Wrap the lead rope around the horse's neck. Stand at the horse's jawline, facing the side of his head. With the hand closest to the horse's head, hold the shank of the lead rope about 1½ feet from the clip. With the other hand, grasp the Handy Stick in the *handshake hold.*

2. Hold the hand with the lead rope up near the horse's eye. Hold the Handy Stick

Correct position of your body, hands, and Handy Stick allows your horse to easily understand your cues.

upright at the middle of the horse's neck (fig. 6.19).

3. Tap the air with both hands, making four tapping motions toward the horse. If he doesn't respond, start tapping his jaw and neck with the same rhythm. Continue building pressure until you get the correct response.

4. Continue tapping with both your hands and the Handy Stick until the horse cor-

rectly disengages his forequarters, one step (fig. 6.20). Immediately rub him to a stop. Rub the same places you have been tapping. Repeat the exercise. Teach it to both sides of the horse.

Common Handler Mistakes

• Asking for too many steps too soon. Be happy with one consistent step at first. Don't ask for two steps if your horse hasn't mastered one yet.

When your horse moves correctly, his front leg nearest you crosses over the other front leg.

- Losing rhythm. Both hands work together, tapping with rhythm. The hand with the lead rope drives the horse's head away, while the hand with the Handy Stick drives the neck and shoulder.
- Tapping the horse right away. Always tap the air first. Give the horse a chance to succeed.
- Nagging. When you tap the horse, be effective.
- Holding the rope too long or too short.

If your rope is too long, the horse will be able to walk away from you and avoid the cue. If it is too short, you will accidentally pull on his head when he starts to yield the forequarters.

- Standing by the horse's shoulder. Standing behind the drive line only encourages the horse to shoot forward, past you. Stay well in front of the shoulder.
- Pushing the horse. If you push on the horse, he will only push against you. You can't

6.21 A–C

If your horse walks forward in avoidance…briskly back him to correct him…

win. Use driving pressure, with rhythm, to encourage the horse to move.

• Chasing the horse. As the horse starts to yield his forequarters, resist the temptation to run and catch up. Ask for a step or two, then rub him to a stop. Later, when the horse understands what is asked of him, follow him in a circle at a walk.

Common Horse Problems

• Walking forward. Immediately back the horse up quite some distance—at least twenty steps. Back him by tapping the rope with the Handy Stick or bumping the halter. Be fairly aggressive, and back him up with energy. Rub him to a stop and begin again. Be sure that you aren't standing too far back, encouraging the horse to go forward (figs. 6.21 A–C).

• Backing-up. Stay in position and continue gentle, rhythmical tapping. Do not try to stop the horse from backing or increase your cue pressure—he is trying to figure out what you want. Increasing the energy will only upset and confuse him. Patiently wait. Be ready to rub him and reward him when he gets it right.

• Bending the head and leaving the shoulder behind. Hold the Handy Stick with the end toward his shoulder. Tap the horse's shoulder, encouraging him to step across.

• Moving the hindquarters toward you instead of pivoting on them. Use the Handy Stick to tap the hindquarters away. Often, a seesaw exercise is effective: disengage the hindquarters four or five steps; yield the forequarters; then disengage the hindquarters again. Continue until your horse understands the difference between moving the front end and moving the back end.

• Stepping behind the outside leg, rather than in front. Do not stop cueing to reward an

...then continue the exercise.

incorrect movement. Move the Handy Stick further back on the horse's neck to encourage him to step forward a bit.

• Sticking his head in the air. Hold both of your hands in the air. If your horse is much taller than you, use your Handy Stick as an extension of your hand, holding it high so the horse can see it.

• Pushing a shoulder into you. Assertively tap the Handy Stick on the shoulder to move him away. If the horse does not respond well, review the four *Backing* exercises (p. 66) before trying again.

Troubleshooting

• If the horse regularly walks forward when asked to yield, position him so that he faces a fence. Use the fence to block his path.

Tips for Success

• Do not try to teach this exercise when the horse is fresh. You will only set him up for failure. Teach it when the horse has shown a willingness to work and you have his attention.

• Some people have better success cueing for this exercise if they hold the Handy Stick horizontally, with one hand on each end.

※ *Cecelia*

"This was a difficult maneuver for me at first. I didn't understand how much to cue the horse on his face. Smacks wanted to walk forward. I had to put my hand up slightly in front of his eyeball in order to stop the forward motion and get him to pay attention to the sideways cue.

"In the beginning, more is not necessarily better. When you get one step, instead of asking for another one immediately, you have to stop and let the horse know he responded correctly.

"The only cue to stop is to rub the horse. It takes a little bit for the horse to figure things out and for the trainer to get the timing right.

"Holding the Handy Stick horizontally with both hands worked best for us since Smacks is so tall and can raise his head up so high. I felt it created a more visible wall to cue him with. We made better progress when I started cueing that way."

※ *Paula*

"So far, this was the hardest exercise for us. I was holding my hand steady near Fancy's face. I had to remember to 'pump' with both hands in rhythm.

"I also had to learn not to be too firm. Now that I have gotten over my timid tendencies, I had to back off a bit on this exercise! The object, Clinton pointed out, is not to slap the horse in the head and neck. Just tap enough to be annoying until the horse moves that one step. Then stop and rub. Then cue again.

"The progress Fancy made once I got my act together was inspiring. When we finally got these first few exercises under better control, after a few days of practice, it was like we were dancing."

Lungeing for Respect—Stage One

6.22

Lungeing for Respect—Stage One teaches the horse to move around you with energy while remaining light on the halter and responsive to your cues.

Tools Needed

Rope halter

14-foot lead rope with duct tape

Handy Stick

String used as a drive line

Goal

To have the horse move out of your *Hula Hoop*, in the direction you choose, and trot energetically around you without pulling on the lead rope. When asked, the horse disengages his hindquarters, stops and turns to face you.

Why Do It?

Riding in Australia, or any other place with wide open spaces, gives you a quick appreciation of the value of lungeing. If a colt is feeling fresh and full of himself, a little lungeing can save you from a long walk home.

Lungeing is an excellent way to get rid of a horse's excess energy. It shows the horse that you can make him move his feet without you moving yours. Lungeing reminds the horse to respond to light pressure. It also gives you more ground control while enforcing the Hula

6.23 A–D

As I'm doing with Fancy, point in the direction you want the horse to travel. Twirl the Handy Stick to cue the horse for impulsion.

Hoop concept. It allows to gauge your horse's temperament and attitude before you get on.

Teaching Steps

1. Stand facing your horse. To lunge counter-clockwise, hold the lead rope with your left hand at the duct tape. With the right hand, grasp the Handy Stick in the *handshake hold*.

2. With your left hand, point up high to your left. If the horse doesn't move, twirl the Handy Stick in three big circles. If the horse still doesn't move, step forward, tap him on the neck and drive him away with the Handy Stick.

3. When the horse faces left, stay behind the drive line. Twirl the Handy Stick toward the horse's hindquarters. Tap, if you need to, until the horse trots forward. When the horse moves, immediately stop cueing.

If the horse doesn't move, tap her neck...
and drive her in the right direction.
Stay behind the drive line as the horse lunges.

*To disengage the
horse's hindquarters
while lungeing:
Slide...Stab...*

A

B

4. Walk a small circle, keeping your belly button facing the horse's head and neck.

5. After the horse trots two or three circles around you, ask him to yield his hind-quarters.

6. Slide your left hand down the rope toward the horse's halter. Pull the rope toward your belly button. Step toward the horse's tail with your right foot and swing the Handy Stick toward his tail in one large circle.

C

Step…Allow the horse to stop and face you.

D

6.25

Firmly tap the horse away if she crowds you like this.

7. When the horse faces you with two eyes, rub him on the face with the Handy Stick. Repeat the exercise in both directions until the horse moves away and disengages his hindquarters when you ask.

Common Handler Mistakes

• Moving around the horse before lungeing. Avoid the temptation to position yourself at the horse's side. Make the horse responsible for moving in the right direction. If you must move, move straight forward, driving the horse's front end away. Remember, whoever moves first, loses.

• Not pointing up in the air with the lead shank. Pointing makes your intentions very clear. It "opens the door" and shows your horse where to go.

• Pointing after the horse moves. **Don't babysit the horse. If you constantly point, he will soon learn to ignore you.**

• Threatening or nagging. Once the horse is moving at the desired speed, keep your hands relaxed and hold the Handy Stick beside you in a neutral position.

• Stepping in front of the drive line. This may cause your horse to stop or turn. Be aware of your body position. Stay behind the drive line to encourage forward motion.

• Allowing the horse to crowd you. If you can touch the horse with the Handy Stick, he is too close, and you run a greater risk of being injured if he kicks out. As a general rule, allow no more than two feet of the tail of the lead rope on the ground while lungeing.

• Letting the horse out too far. Especially in the beginning, this allows the horse to ignore the cue to disengage his hindquarters. Try to keep about two feet of the lead rope's tail on the ground.

• Pulling the horse in to face you. Concentrate on pushing the hindquarters away. Use the lead rope only to enforce the disengage.

• Taking a small step to disengage. Exaggerate the step toward the horse's tail. Refine the cue only after the horse understands what is expected of him.

Common Horse Problems

• Running backward or sideways when asked to lunge. Swing the Handy Stick. Continue pointing in the direction you want the horse to go. Maintain the cues, but be ready to take the pressure off as soon as the horse moves in the right direction.

• Trying to get to the gate or near other horses. Lunge the horse right next to the arena gate or his friends. Let him rest away from the "magnet." Soon, the attraction will fade.

• Rearing. Ignore this behavior and keep applying pressure. If necessary, put the string on the end of the Handy Stick in order to be able to reach the horse without endangering yourself.

• Pinning his ears or crowding toward you. Step forward and spank the horse on the side of the neck with the Handy Stick (fig. 6.25). Recognize his bad behavior as an insult and refuse to accept it. Make him uncomfortable for being disrespectful.

• Laziness at the trot. Point. If the horse doesn't speed up, cluck to him. If the horse still doesn't speed up, spank him with the Handy Stick. If the horse is really lazy, have him canter the circle. Then trotting will look easy.

• Kicking out. Put the string on the Handy Stick. Every time the horse kicks out, spank him on the top of his tail. Be very clear that such behavior will not be ignored.

• Not yielding the hindquarters. Slide your hand further down the lead rope, toward the horse's head. "Stab yourself" in the belly button with the rope hand. Step in toward the hindquarters again, and swing the Handy Stick in a large circle. Continue until the horse faces you. If necessary, review *Disengage and Turn to Face You* (see p. 63).

• Anticipating the yield. Do the opposite of what the horse expects. If he starts to disengage his hindquarters before you tell him to, continue lungeing in a circle.

Troubleshooting

• If you have a lazy horse, get his feet moving. Have him trot around longer before asking for the disengage.

• Hotter horses that want to run benefit from frequent disengages with shorter trotting periods between them.

Tips for Success

• When swinging the Handy Stick toward the horse's tail to disengage the hindquarters, use an overhand motion, as if serving a tennis ball.

• Always step toward the tail using the foot on the same side as the Handy Stick.

• Cue with the Handy Stick toward the neck for direction. Then cue the hindquarters for impulsion. Pointing gives direction. The Handy Stick provides the reason to go.

• When using the string on the end of your Handy Stick, don't flick it like a whip. Always cue by swinging the Handy Stick forward and around in a circle.

❋ *Cecelia*

"I love the string around the horse's neck defining the drive line. It makes it easier to keep myself in the right position. Clinton says if you drive the butt, the horse will go. He's right. The drive line helps ensure the handler's success.

"I liked not clucking or flicking a whip to keep the horse trotting. 'Point, cluck, spank'

makes the horse responsible for his behavior, instead of nagging at him the whole time.

"I had written Smacks off as a hunter prospect. I had never seen any signs that he had the mind for it. After working on today's exercises (*Backing, Yielding the Forequarters,* and *Lungeing for Respect—Stage One*), I have changed my tune. Maybe he has it in him."

❋ *Paula*

"Hand placement on the rope—getting the right spot and the right position—is important. Without it, you can't give the cues correctly.

"It really helped when Clinton said to keep about two feet of the lead-rope tail on the ground. That was a useful way to gauge my distance from the horse.

"Fancy would have run me over just a few days ago if I had asked her to lunge. Our way of lungeing was me chasing her around with a whip. Now there is such a difference in her attitude. The change in her after learning only a few exercises is almost unbelievable."

Flexing to the Halter

Flexing to the Halter makes the horse light and supple.

Tools Needed

Rope halter

14-foot lead rope

For this exercise, position the halter slightly lower on the horse's nose than usual. This will make it easier for your horse to understand your cues. It will also make it more difficult for your horse to pull against you or ignore you.

Goal

To lightly pick up the lead rope and have the horse soften to pressure and touch his side with his nose while keeping his feet still.

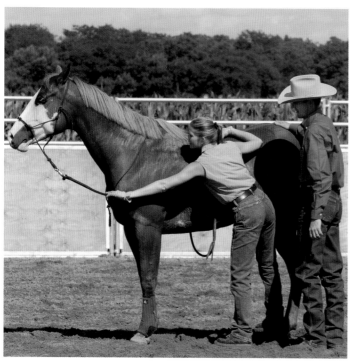

6.27 A–D

Stand close to the horse's flank when grasping the lead rope. Pull the rope to the horse's withers. When the horse gives to pressure…release immediately.

Why Do It?

Flexing to the Halter not only increases a horse's suppleness, it also builds a foundation for flexibility and direction control under saddle. If the horse flexes well from the ground, you will have little problem flexing him under saddle.

Teaching Steps

1. Stand by your horse's flank, with your belly button facing him. "Hug" your horse, putting the arm closest to the tail over his hips or hindquarters. Fold the lead rope in half and drape it over his back.

2. Slide the other hand down the lead rope to about 2½ feet from the clip. Pull the lead rope to the horse's withers, bending his head toward you.

3. As soon as the horse gives to the pressure, creating slack in the lead rope, and his feet don't move, quickly drop the rope and reward him. Repeat several times on both sides.

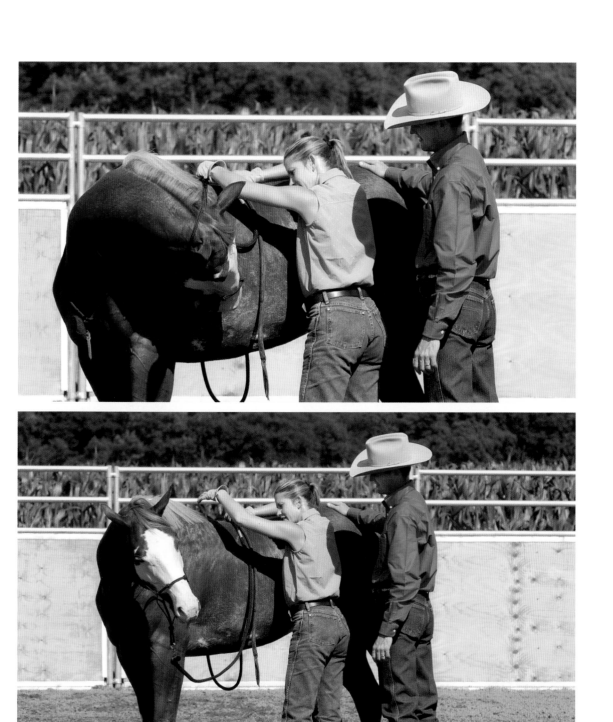

Common Handler Mistakes

• Standing too far forward. **Stay by the flank. Standing close to the shoulder does not allow enough space for the horse to turn his head and yield to the pressure you create. You also run a greater risk of the horse stepping on your foot.**

• Drawing the rope over the horse's back. **Keep your hand on the side you stand. Don't let the cueing hand cross over the horse's spine.**

• Holding your hand up in the air. **Keep your hand beside the horse's withers. This will give you stability and you will be able to recognize the slightest try on his part. If necessary, put both hands on the rope.**

• Releasing too slowly when the horse gives. **The quicker you release the pressure, the sooner your horse will learn the lesson.**

• Pulling the horse's head all the way around. **Only pull the horse's head about three-quarters of the way around. Let him decide to yield the rest of the way. This keeps your horse light and ensures that you don't get into a pulling contest with him.**

• Not allowing the horse to straighten his neck between exercises. **Let the horse straighten his neck and head for five seconds or so after he has flexed. This rewards him and provides an incentive for him to flex the next time you ask. When you release, make sure that the rope has enough slack so there is no tension on the horse's head.**

• Releasing the rope in order to tighten it. **If you need to tighten the lead rope, keep it taut with the hand on the withers. Pull the rope through with the other hand.**

• Jerking on the rope. **Resist the temptation to jerk on the horse's head. Follow the steps, and be patient.**

• Falling out of position when the horse moves. **Hug the hindquarters to help keep you in the correct position. Keep your cueing hand firmly on the withers. Stay with the horse until his feet stop and he softens toward you.**

Common Horse Problems

• Walking around or backing-up. **Your horse may try to move away from the cue at first. Do not correct him. Stay in position until his feet stop and he softens toward you.**

• Leaning on the halter. **Again, there is seldom a need for correction. Anchor your cueing hand securely beside his withers and wait. If the horse actually falls asleep, however, bump him in the belly with your knee and wake him up a bit.**

• Smelling you. **The horse may be more interested in smelling you than in flexing and giving to the pressure. Wait patiently until he makes the correct decision.**

• Softening, but nibbling on his side or belly. **In the early stages, as long as the horse doesn't bite _you_, ignore this behavior. Allow him to rest, then continue the exercise.**

Troubleshooting

• If the horse doesn't seem to understand the concept, make sure your lead rope isn't too short. The object is not to pull the horse's head all the way around to his body.

• If the horse understands the concept early in the lesson but gets less and less responsive, you are probably releasing the pressure too slowly. Drop the lead rope and give immediate relief when the horse flexes and softens.

Tips for Success

Remember to reward the slightest try. You can eventually ask for more and more flex until the horse touches his side with his nose. At first, however, release as soon as the horse willingly yields to the pressure, creating slack in the lead rope.

• Repetition keeps the horse light. For an easy way to work this exercise into your daily routine, flex the horse at least five times on each side every time you catch him.

✳ *Cecelia*

"I have done some similar exercises with Smacks before. I was pleased: he flexed to the halter very well.

"I had to be careful, however, not to pull the horse's head all the way into position. Clinton told me to pull his head only three-quarters of the way. It was up to Smacks to finish the job.

"Smacks went through a phase when he shook his head, trying to get out of doing the work. He has a history of doing the same thing under saddle and ripping the reins out of my hands. Clinton pointed out that Smacks was acting very disrespectfully. He told me to do a series of bumps and create some energy on the halter every time Smacks got 'snakey.' It didn't take long before the horse stopped shaking his head."

✳ *Paula*

"At first, Fancy wasn't really trying. She wasn't pulling against me much, but she also wasn't making any effort to yield to the halter. I had to tighten the lead rope and ask for more in order to make it worth her while to give. I got her to give a little bit more each time until I had her cooperation.

"Since I'm not very tall, I literally had to have my stomach touch the horse when I asked her to flex. That was the only way I could get in the correct position and stay there.

"I was just amazed at how quickly we made progress. The second day, Fancy was a whole lot better. She was much softer and flexed so much more easily."

6.28

Sending is a good way to control the horse's feet while keeping him focused on you.

*The horse must master **Disengage the Hindquarters** (p. 60) and **Lungeing for Respect—Stage One** (p. 83) before being taught **Sending**.*

Tools Needed

Rope halter
14-foot lead rope with duct tape
Handy Stick
String used as a drive line
Sturdy, safe section of fence

Goal

To have your horse go through a tight, narrow space without his feeling claustrophobic or panicking.

Why Do It?

Horses working in Australia must regularly navigate tight spaces. They need to easily load onto stock trailers or cattle trucks. They should also calmly walk through narrow gates or chutes when working cattle. *Sending* accustoms the horse to being in tight, narrow, claustrophobic spaces without panicking.

Use Sending for teaching trailer loading, navigating puddles, walking past scary banners—the practical applications are endless. If you can "send" the horse between you and

Sending is an excellent exercise to help your horse overcome a fear of spooky objects.

something scary, you will have much better control of him in many more situations.

Teaching Steps

1. Stand about 15 feet away from a fence, facing the fence. Hold the lead rope and Handy Stick as you did in *Lungeing for Respect—Stage One.* Hold the lead rope at the duct tape.

2. With the hand holding the lead rope, point high in the direction you want the horse to go—between you and the fence (figs. 6.30 A–D). If the horse doesn't walk forward, use the Handy Stick to gently tap the air beside him. If he doesn't respond, tap him with rhythm behind the drive line.

3. As soon as the horse's hindquarters pass you, pull the rope hand toward your belly button. With the opposite foot, step forward toward the horse's tail. At the same time, swing the Handy Stick in a large, overhand circle, asking the horse to disengage his hindquarters and face you.

4. Allow the horse to rest a few seconds. Switch hands with the lead rope and Handy Stick. "Send" the horse between you and the fence the other way. Disengage his hindquarters as soon as they pass you. Teach the exercise at a walk and a trot.

5. When your horse is comfortable going through the 15-foot gap, gradually work your way closer to the fence. Eventually, the horse should "send" through a three-foot gap between you and the fence.

6.30 A–D

Point in the direction you want to "send" the horse. When the hindquarters pass you, step toward the horse's tail, "stab" your belly button, and swing the Handy Stick overhand… disengaging the horse's hindquarters. Then "send" your horse back the way he came.

A

B

C

D

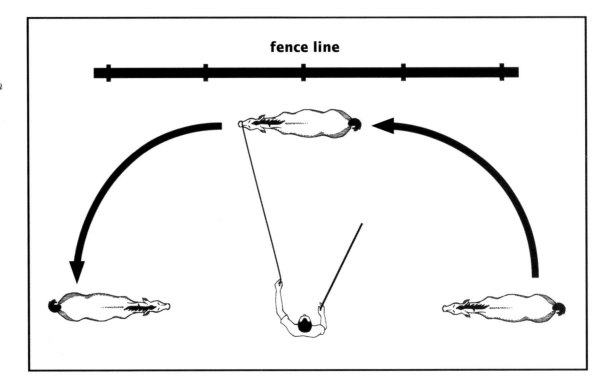

fence line

Common Handler Mistakes

• Starting too close to the fence. **Start back far enough so that the horse doesn't feel trapped or closed-in.**

• Not pointing. **You must clearly indicate the direction you want the horse to go.**

• Waiting too long to disengage the hind-quarters. **As you face the fence, imagine a line from your belly button to the fence. When the horse's hindquarters pass that line, take one giant step forward, as if you were going to step on his tail. Remember to step with the foot on the same side as the hand that holds the Handy Stick.**

• Not letting the horse rest. **Every time you yield the horse's hindquarters, rub him on the face with the Handy Stick, desensitizing**

him a bit before repeating the exercise.

• Moving your feet too much. **Ideally, your feet should pivot 180 degrees as the horse trots a series of arcs between you and the fence. Take a large step to disengage the hindquarters. Then, return to your original position (fig. 6.31).**

Common Horse Problems

• Backing up when asked to send. **Follow the horse, maintaining the cues. Stay calm and stay with him until he responds correctly.**

• Anticipating. **After several Sending exercises, some horses will start to anticipate what comes next. Make the horse pause and wait for you to "send" him through. You may want to back him up a few strides.**

- Ambling. If your horse walks lazily through the exercise, have him do it at a trot a few times. Tap with the Handy Stick to encourage him to move with energy.
- Running around behind you. Give the cue to disengage the hindquarters as soon as the horse's tail passes in front of you. If you wait until the horse has already gone between you and the fence, you have waited too long—his momentum will carry him behind you.
- Crowding. If the horse crowds you as you "send" him through the gap, tap him smartly on the neck with rhythm to encourage him to stay away. If he crowds into you after disengaging the hindquarters, use the Handy Stick to reinforce your *Hula Hoop* space.
- Kicking out. If you crowd the horse too close to the fence too soon, he may feel claustrophobic or trapped. A panicking horse is a dangerous one. If he kicks in aggression, use the Handy Stick on his hindquarters to sharply disengage them. Continue the exercise until his attitude improves.
- Racing through. If your horse charges through the opening between you and the fence, have him do the exercise continuously, until he relaxes and walks.

Troubleshooting

- If the horse ignores your cue to disengage, do a few short bumps on the lead rope, and whack his hindquarters firmly to encourage a snappy disengage. If necessary, review *Lungeing for Respect—Stage One* (p. 83).

Tips for Success

- Some horses are very claustrophobic. In these cases, you may have to start even more than 15 feet away from the fence.

- Take your time; don't rush. The goal is to have your horse calmly walk or trot between you and an obstacle.

❊ Cecelia

"What helped me was to slow the process down. I was getting too aggressive. It helped to have Smacks just walk the exercise a few times. I appreciated Clinton telling me that the object wasn't to do it fast.

"One morning, a tractor dragged the arena while we were working. We did this exercise a few times and that was all that I needed to keep Smacks' attention on me. He looked at the tractor a little. But he paid attention to me! It was like owning a different horse!"

❊ Paula

"I asked Fancy to go too fast at first. Clinton reminded me that this exercise wasn't about speed. I don't want her to go flying between me and the wall. I want her to walk or trot quietly and calmly.

"It wasn't as easy to get her to yield the hindquarters as it was when lungeing. Even though she moved slower, it all seemed to happen faster, since I had to disengage her hindquarters every half-circle. I really had to concentrate to get my cues right.

"I started out applying too much pressure and caused Fancy to back up. When she didn't go forward like I wanted, I increased the pressure, which only made her go backward faster. Clinton told me to keep my cue consistent until the horse gave me the desired response (going forward). He explained that increasing the pressure when she didn't understand only made her more concerned about the pressure and less able to figure out what I wanted."

6.32

Circle Driving builds fluidity and responsiveness.

Tools Needed
    Rope halter
    14-foot lead rope with duct tape
    Handy Stick

Goal
    To have the horse trot in a circle beside you, within touching distance, on a slack lead line; to change directions fluidly, without crowding the handler or stopping the forward motion.

Why Do It?
    Circle Driving teaches the horse not to push into your space. It also teaches him not to pull away. He learns to focus on you and pay greater attention to your body language.

Stage One—Establish a Consistent Circle

Teaching Steps
1. With your left hand, hold the lead line at the duct tape. With your right hand, use the Handy Stick in the *handshake hold*. Face left (counterclockwise).
2. Walk forward. Point, with your lead-rope hand, in the direction you are facing. If the horse doesn't trot up beside you, reach back

6.33

*When **Circle Driving**,
the horse learns to
stay soft on the halter
and bend in an arc
around you.*

and tap him on the withers until he does.

3. With the horse trotting beside you, walk a
10-foot circle. Rest the Handy Stick on the
horse's withers. Keep the horse's shoulder
in line with yours (fig. 6.33).

4. Whenever the horse lags behind you, point
first with the lead rope, then tap him on the
withers until he comes forward into position.

5. After a few good circles, turn and step
toward the horse's hindquarters. Swing the
Handy Stick in a large overhand circle
toward the hindquarters, asking the horse
to disengage. Tap the hindquarters if the
horse doesn't disengage (figs. 6.34 A–D).

6. Allow the horse to stand for a few seconds.
Rub him with the Handy Stick. Face left
again, and continue Circle Driving in the
same direction. After the horse masters Circle Driving on one side, change sides. Hold
the lead rope in your right hand and the
Handy Stick in your left to go clockwise.

Common Handler Mistakes

• Waiting for the horse before walking forward. You determine the beginning of the
exercise. Walk. Point. Tap. Walk in a straight
line until the horse comes up beside you, then
begin your circle.

6.34 A–D

To begin, walk forward. Point where you want to go. Continue facing forward. When the horse trots up beside you, place the Handy Stick on his withers and begin circling. Turn...step...swing ...and disengage the horse's hindquarters.

- Facing the horse. Circle Driving is not lungeing. Keep your belly button facing *forward*, in the direction you are going.
- Walking too slowly. Walking at a brisk, comfortable pace will encourage your horse to trot around you in a circle.
- Not walking in a circle. As soon as the horse is beside you, begin to walk in a circle. This encourages him to bend his body and arc around you.
- Pointing when the horse is already moving. Pointing is the "go" cue. When the horse moves at the correct speed, stop pointing and put your hand on your belly button.
- Not pointing before tapping. Tap the horse with the Handy Stick only after he has not responded to your more subtle direction cue.
- Not resting the Handy Stick on the horse's withers. As the horse trots along, keep the Handy Stick in place on his withers. This provides an easy reference for you to tell if the horse is too close, or too far away.

Common Horse Problems

- Crowding too close. If the Handy Stick is more than three inches on the other side of the horse's spine, he is too close. Tap him on the side of the neck to move him out a bit.
- Nervousness. Some horses may not like the feel of the Handy Stick on their withers at first. Stay calm and continue the exercise until the horse relaxes. If the horse gets more nervous, review *Desensitizing to the Handy Stick and String—Stage One* (p. 55).
- Trotting too fast. Walk a smaller circle so you don't have to cover as much ground to keep up. Disengage the hindquarters more frequently. The horse will soon realize that he is getting nowhere in a hurry.

- Trotting too slowly. Point in the direction you are going, then tap the Handy Stick behind the horse's withers to cue him to speed up and stay with you.

Troubleshooting

- If the horse insists on crowding you, use the Handy Stick to firmly tap his belly. This will keep him from pushing on you. It will also encourage him to arc his barrel away and bend his body from head to tail.

Tips for Success

- Follow your belly button: keep it facing forward in the direction you are walking.

❈ *Cecelia*

"It took a little bit for me to get the hang of walking a circle while facing forward instead of facing my horse. This is a very different exercise from lungeing, but old habits die hard.

"I really relied on the duct tape on the lunge line. It was a good reference point so I knew where my hand should be.

"I got 'tap happy.' I had to tell myself to point first to give Smacks the chance to go forward on his own.

"Smacks wanted to get a little sloppy when I asked him to yield the hindquarters. Clinton told me to make sure the horse faced me with two eyes and two ears. I saw, once we moved on to *Stage Two*, how important it was to get the disengage correct.

"Circle Driving makes the horse so soft. But it is a completely sequential process. You can't do this exercise correctly until the horse has gotten all of the other ground exercises up until this point. Don't skip steps A and B to get to C."

❋ Paula

"Determining where to tap is important. Don't tap on the topline or on the mane. Tap on the side of the horse's withers.

"I had to remember to point before I tapped. Once Fancy was trotting, however, I sometimes forgot to lower the arm with the rope and ended up pulling or dragging her.

"Clinton reminded me not to walk straight for very long. We weren't practicing leading. As soon as Fancy started to get up beside me, I was to get her circling."

Stage Two—Change Directions

Teaching Steps

1. Begin with *Stage One.* After a few good circles, disengage the horse's hindquarters.
2. Keep your feet still. Pass the Handy Stick under the lead rope and change hands.
3. Look straight ahead. Choose an object in front of you and take three steps toward it.
4. Point up high in the air and encourage the horse to trot up beside you.
5. As soon as the horse is even with your shoulder, rest the Handy Stick on his withers and begin circling in the new direction.
6. Continue the exercise until the horse changes directions fluidly. Once you have mastered the steps, practice changing directions without stopping your feet (figs. 6.35 A–D).

Common Handler Mistakes

• Waiting for the horse before walking forward. As soon as the horse's hindquarters begin to disengage, change hands with the Handy Stick and lead rope and begin walking in the new direction.

• Not walking straight forward in the new direction. When you step to disengage the horse's hindquarters, consider that your first step in the new direction. Continue in a straight line until the horse comes up beside you. *Then* circle.

Common Horse Problems

• Resisting against halter pressure when asked to come forward. Tap the Handy Stick behind the withers to bring the horse up beside you.

Troubleshooting

• If you have difficulty mastering *Stage Two*, practice changing hands with the lead rope and Handy Stick several times without putting the horse into the equation. Be able to smoothly and quickly change hands before trying the exercise again. Always move the Handy Stick underneath the rope when changing hands.

Tips for Success

• After yielding the hindquarters, choose a point in front of you and walk straight toward it, until the horse comes up beside you. Walk at your normal pace.

• Keep your movements quiet and deliberate. Don't rush. At the end of this exercise, you should not feel as if you have run a marathon.

❋ Cecelia

"Smacks is getting so much more responsive and willing. I couldn't be happier with the progress he is making. There is a lot to think about on my part, though: changing hands, disengaging correctly, and continuing to walk when changing directions.

"The comfort level is an issue as well.

6.35 A–D

Establish a circle in one direction… disengage the horse's hindquarters, walk straight ahead… and establish a circle in the new direction.

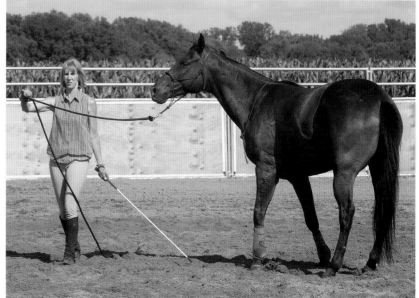

These exercises are intense. There is nothing wimpy about them. You can't teach them all at once: your body couldn't take it.

"I was a little intimidated to try this exercise because I didn't know exactly what to expect from it. Once we got working, however, I could see that it was not 'new'. It builds on what we already know.

"I like the fact that Clinton's whole approach is focused on success. It is wonderful, because the success is measurable. I have so many new tools now. Even if I am not great at it, I still make progress."

✳ Paula

"In order to change directions, I had a tough time remembering to turn toward the horse before stepping forward to disengage the hindquarters (Step 5 of *Stage One*). I also had to constantly remind myself to ask for the disengage using the foot on the same side of my body as the Handy Stick. It got me off balance at first.

"Fancy tends to be lazy, but it didn't take her long to understand that I didn't nag at her when she stayed with me. I was surprised at how quickly she picked this up. I know it is because of all the exercises we have done up to this point. There is no way we could have started with this one."

6.36

Lungeing for
Respect—Stage Two
teaches the horse to
be light in front while
using his
hindquarters for
energetic changes of
direction.

Tools Needed
Rope halter
14-foot lead rope
Handy Stick
String used as a drive line

Goal
To have the horse circle around you, roll back 180 degrees on his hindquarters, and move off energetically in the opposite direction.

Why Do It?
This exercise will give you more control of the horse's front end. It encourages the horse to be lighter and teaches him greater agility.

In order to do this exercise correctly, the horse must pay close attention to the handler's cues. This is an excellent way to get the horse to quickly focus on you.

Teaching Steps
1. Hold the lead rope and Handy Stick as you did for *Stage One*. Ask the horse to circle around you two or three times at a trot.
2. Before asking for a change of direction, turn the hand holding the lead rope palm up, with the last three fingers of the hand under the rope. Put the Handy Stick in this hand.
3. Slide the free hand down the rope, toward the horse (fig. 6.37 A).

Slide your free hand down the rope...step in front of the drive line...then point to clearly signal a change of direction.

4. Take one big step sideways, out in front of the drive line. Point up high in the new direction you want the horse to go. Twirl the Handy Stick. Tap the horse, if necessary, until the horse moves off in the new direction. Lunge the horse at a trot for two or three circles before asking for another direction change (figs. 6.37 B & C).

Taking a giant step sideways, in front of the drive line encourages the horse to stop her forward movement and expend her energy in a new direction.

Common Handler Mistakes

• Holding the rope incorrectly. Point your thumb toward you and your little finger toward the horse. This helps you give a better direction cue. It also enables you to hold onto the rope more effectively if the horse tries to pull against you.

• Forgetting the correct cues to change directions. If you are having trouble, practice the steps without the horse. Say the steps out loud to yourself until they are firmly in your mind. As you gain confidence, start blending the steps together.

• Not stepping in front of the horse. Step in front of where the horse *will be* (figs. 6.38 A–C). If you try to step in front of where he *is*, it will seem that you are running at him. His natural reaction will be to either turn away or run past you.

• Holding the rope too long or too short. Keep about a foot of the rope's tail on the ground while lungeing. Slide your hand as far up the rope as possible before cueing for the change of direction. Remember to let the rope slide through your hands again after the horse has changed.

Common Horse Problems

• Speeding up when you step to change directions. Bump repeatedly on the lead shank until the horse's head turns in the right direction. Then twirl or tap the Handy Stick, until he moves forward.

• Pivoting on the front end or doing a U-turn. Firmly tap the horse's shoulder with the Handy Stick to encourage him to pick up his front end and use his hindquarters more.

Troubleshooting

• To avoid getting the Handy Stick tangled in the lead rope when changing hands, always pass it underneath the rope.

Tips for Success

• Remember: direction before impulsion. Swing the Handy Stick toward the horse's head and neck to get him facing in the right direction. Then, swing it toward the hindquarters to add impulsion.

✳ *Cecelia*

"A few times, Smacks thought he was going to leave me. I bumped on the lead rope until he realized it was in his best interest to pay attention to me.

"Clinton reminded me not to keep constant pressure on the rope. I don't want to drag the horse around me. I have to drive him forward.

"Smacks had a ton of resistance through his head and neck. He had to learn to associate moving his feet forward to release pressure on his poll.

"I had to remember to use my whole arm to twirl the Handy Stick. I wanted to twirl it using just my hand and wrist, but it didn't take long before the stick gets very heavy. Using my whole arm saved my wrist. It also made my cue clearer to Smacks.

"Clinton reminded us to take a *big* step sideways. That equals a dramatic step in front of the drive line, and stops the horse's forward motion.

"It helped me enormously to practice changing hands with the lead rope and Handy Stick without actually asking the horse to change direction. On this exercise, after a bit, my brain was getting full. Clinton had us say the steps over and over while we did them. But I got to the point where I couldn't even think of the next step. Until I got the feel for it, I really had to concentrate on doing it right.

"It wasn't pretty in the beginning. But the more changes of direction we did, the better they got."

✳ *Paula*

"While we were lungeing, Clinton told me to pull and release on the rope to get Fancy's head tipped toward me. I had to get her attention, drive her on, and not let her ignore me.

"Clinton made us say the steps for changing direction out loud, over and over again, while we did them. I'm thankful that he did that. It really helped cement the steps in my mind.

"I need to remember to keep my belly button facing behind the drive line. I kept wanting to face too far forward, which gave conflicting signals about whether I wanted my horse to go forward or turn.

"For a while, Fancy tried to do what Clinton called a 'screaming U-turn.' He pointed out that the goal of the exercise was not to have the horse run me over. I used the Handy Stick to make it worth her while to stay out of my space. When she saw that I was serious, she really used herself. She rocked back on her hind end and pivoted around. I was amazed.

"I got dragged off my feet a couple of times because I didn't let the rope slide through my hands when Fancy changed directions. When you slide your hand forward to change directions, you have shortened the rope. Remember to let it slide through your hands and go back to the original length."

Leading Beside

6.38

Leading Beside *teaches the horse to take responsibility for staying with you.*

Tools Needed

Rope halter
14-foot lead rope
Handy Stick
String used as a guide line
Sturdy fence line

Goal

To lead your horse beside you at a walk and trot on a slack lead. To have the horse act as your shadow, going where you go, at your speed, turning when you turn, and stopping when you stop.

Why Do It?

Every horse should lead safely and quietly.

One of the few things that irritates Australian horsemen more than having a horse drag behind them is a horse that runs them over. They spend too much time handling horses from the ground to tolerate disrespect from a horse that doesn't lead well.

In many ways, having a horse that leads quietly and respectfully, shadowing your every move, is a matter of pride. Nothing could more clearly show the horse's respect for you and desire to be with you.

6.39 A

*Hold the lead rope
about an elbow's
length from the
snap.*

Teaching Steps

Stage One—Follow the Fence

1. Stand on the left side of your horse, parallel to the fence, with your horse between you and the fence. Keep your shoulder even with the guide line. Hold the lead rope in your right hand (fig. 6.39 A). Use the Handy Stick in the *handshake hold* with your left hand

2. Walk forward. If your horse lags behind, stretch your right arm out in front of you, pointing with the lead rope where you want to go.

3. If the horse doesn't come forward immediately, reach behind you with the Handy Stick (fig. 6.39 B).

4. If the horse walks too fast and the guide line gets in front of you, turn to the inside (left) and walk a small circle. Continue along the fence in the original direction.

5. Continue until the horse consistently stays in position at your side.

6.39 B

Tap the horse until the guide line is even with your shoulder.

6.40

Walk in an arc when turning to the outside. Use your arm and Handy Stick as needed to push the horse out of your space.

Stage Two—Inside Turns

1. When your horse leads well along the fence, turn left (away from your horse) 90 degrees. Walk in a straight line for 5 to 10 strides. Turn left again and make another inside turn.

2. Continue doing inside turns every 10 strides or so until the horse stays with you consistently.

Stage Three—Outside Turns

1. While walking, turn 90 degrees to the outside (right). Raise both hands and tap the air toward your horse's head to encourage him to move away (fig. 6.40).

2. If the horse pushes into you, put your right arm up by his eye to block him. If necessary, bump on his jaw to push him away from you.

3. Once the horse understands what is asked of him, start alternating inside and outside turns.

4. Practice all three stages from both sides of the horse.

IMPORTANT NOTE
••••••••

*Do not practice **Stage Three** until you and your horse have mastered **Stages One and Two** as well as **Yielding the Forequarters** (p. 77).*

6.41

*When trotting, the
horse should stay in
position at your side
with no tension on
the lead rope.*

Stage Four—Trotting

1. Begin walking the horse beside the fence, as in *Stage One*. When the horse is leading well, lean your body forward. Stretch out the hand with the lead rope and point in the direction you want to go.
2. If the horse doesn't trot, reach back and tap him with the Handy Stick.
3. When the horse begins trotting, start to jog. If the horse trots too fast, do small circles to the inside, as in Step 4 of *Stage One*.
4. Follow the stages, first teaching the horse to trot along the fence. Next, teach inside turns. Finish with outside turns. Practice *Leading Beside* at the trot from both sides of the horse (fig. 6.41).

Common Handler Mistakes

• Incorrect body position. Keep your shoulder even with the guide line around your horse's neck. This will help keep you from falling too far back or walking too far out in front.

• Bending the arm with the Handy Stick. When you reach behind to tap the horse, keep

6.42

Point to cue the horse that you want to speed up.

your entire arm straight. Bending your arm makes it difficult to tap the horse.

• Not pointing before tapping. Give the horse the opportunity to respond to the subtler cue (fig. 6.42).

• Turning more than 90 degrees. In the beginning, keep your turns to a quarter of a circle until the horse has mastered all four stages. Make it possible for your horse to do well with the exercise.

• Walking too slowly. Walk at your normal pace. Teach the horse to rate his speed to stay with you (fig. 6.43).

Common Horse Problems

• Running forward or trotting when asked to walk. Be certain you aren't pointing or giving any other cue for the horse to speed up. Walk a small circle, and wait until he slows down, then continue in the original direction. Walk as many small circles as necessary. Eventually, the horse will realize that charging ahead of you doesn't get him anywhere.

• Lagging behind. This is very common when first teaching inside turns. Lean forward a bit. Point where you are going and tap the horse with your Handy Stick.

6.43

Walk at a comfortable pace without dragging or nagging your horse.

• Inconsistency. Some horses lag behind, then charge forward, overcompensating. Be patient. Keep your walking, pointing, and tapping cues clear.

Troubleshooting

• If you have trouble negotiating outside turns, review *Yielding the Forequarters* (p. 77) until the horse responds better when asked to move out of your space

Tips for Success

• Keep the lead rope slack. Once the horse has learned Leading Beside, practice every time you lead him. This exercise is a very good way to teach a horse to pay attention to subtle body language.

※ *Cecelia*

"Clinton reminded me not to get too close to the fence. I didn't want to make Smacks feel trapped while we practiced this.

"Before we learned this exercise, Smacks had the tendency to drag me wherever he wanted when I led him. I would hold him up close to his halter and constantly either pull on him or redirect him. Now, he understands that he is responsible for his actions. He is a much quieter, more confident horse.

"This exercise is all about body language. We exaggerated it at first, but it was very effective. To trot, I leaned forward as if I was going to run. I would point before I tapped him. Pointing gave Smacks a chance to stay with me. When he got where I wanted him, I would relax back to a normal body position. It didn't take long before he started watching for my signals.

"Don't be in a hurry to change directions. A few times, I would pivot suddenly, and Smacks would be totally unprepared for the turn. When I made my turns more gradually, I could concentrate on my horse. It became more reasonable to expect him to keep up with me.

"Practice a lot of transitions from trot to walk. At first, Smacks wanted to jump forward into the trot. Since he was doing what I asked, I would jog in a fairly small circle until he got the hang of staying beside me. It was less work for me while I allowed him to find his stride.

"The key for us was not to trot too long, at first. We would just do a few steps. Then, we would walk again. That way, he didn't get too far in front of me, and I didn't run out of breath."

✳ *Paula*

"Using the guide line as a visual aid was very helpful to keep me in position.

"We practiced this exercise quite a while. It was important to find a pace that I could keep up. Don't charge forward—you will get tired too quickly. And don't drag—you will bore both of you.

"Remember to lean forward and point before using the Handy Stick to tap. Give the horse a chance to make the right choice. But don't hesitate to follow up if she doesn't stay with you.

"Immediately after learning this, I used it when I went to wash Fancy. She used to walk into me or shoulder me out of her way. Not any more. I am going to use this from now on. Fancy will always lead this way."

7

RIDING TOOLS

Whether you prefer to ride English or Western style, the basic training tools remain the same. Safety, convenience, and effectiveness are key factors.

Every combination of rider, horse, and tack is different. As with the chapter on *Groundwork Tools*, I have included a list of what I consider essential aids for teaching mounted exercises. While you may substitute different equipment, it may take longer to achieve the desired results under saddle.

Here are some of the tools I prefer when teaching *Essential Exercises Under Saddle* (p. 135).

Saddle

The training saddle should be clean, sturdy, and well-fitted to you and your horse. Be sure the stirrups are well maintained and wide enough for your foot to easily slip in and out. Keep all leather parts well oiled. Pay special attention to the care and cleaning of your girth.

※ *Paula*

"My saddle was too small for me. Before I went to work with Clinton, I hadn't spent enough time in it to know that. It didn't take too long for Clinton to point out that it didn't fit me at all. Being saddle-sore is no laughing matter, especially when you have several more hours of riding ahead of you."

Bridle

As with the saddle, your training bridle should be clean, sturdy, and well-fitting. Avoid cracked leather or flimsy materials. If your bridle uses screws for fastening the bit and reins, periodically check that the screws are tight.

Reins

Loop reins are ideal for training. They eliminate the risk that a rein will fall to the ground in the middle of an exercise. When the reins are placed over the horse's head to rest

7.1
Ready to ride: training snaffle, mecate reins, well-fitting saddle and bridle and protective boots set the stage for a productive training session.

Cecelia works Smacks in English tack with her "string" for added impulsion and duct tape on the reins as a visual aid. A helmet and boots provide extra protection.

Paula rides Fancy in a Western saddle, mecate reins with duct tape, a snaffle bit for training, and gloves and boots for protection.

on his neck in front of the withers, they should hang loosely.

I prefer mecate reins for most training. The reins are, in essence, a long rope that attaches in a loop to the bit, with the remainder of the rope left to hang free. When not in use, this free end can be wrapped around the saddle horn of a Western saddle. It can be used as tie rope when on a trail ride. When swung gently overhand, from side-to-side, the mecate tail is also a useful way to encourage the horse's impulsion.

Snaffle Bit

I use a snaffle bit on all my horses for training and riding. I recommend a smooth snaffle with a single joint for most training.

Regardless of whether you intend to ultimately ride the horse in English or Western tack, starting with a snaffle simplifies the entire training process. Used correctly, it helps make the horse lighter, more flexible, and more responsive.

Bit adjustment is extremely important. A bit is too tight if it pulls "wrinkles" at the corners of the horse's mouth. The bit is too loose if it hangs in the mouth without touching the corners.

Ideally, the bit should be adjusted so that there is almost one wrinkle in the mouth. This makes it possible for all pressure to release when the horse responds, but keeps the bit high enough to prevent the horse from getting his tongue over it.

I recommend using a leather curb strap on the bit. A curb strap helps keep the bit situated correctly and makes it difficult to pull the bit out of the mouth. Adjust the strap loosely enough to allow several fingers to fit between

it and the horse's jaw. It should not be so loose that it hangs down around the horse's lips.

Bits with shanks are not recommended for any of the exercises covered in this book. Once the exercises have been mastered using a snaffle, changing to a shank bit will simply give greater leverage and control.

I also recommend the following equipment:

Helmet

Regardless of your riding experience, working around horses carries inherent dangers. A well-fitting safety helmet that meets current specifications for equine activities can significantly reduce the risks of severe head injuries.

String

The same six-foot rope string you used for the *Groundwork Exercises* (p. 35) also comes in handy when riding. If mecate reins are not used, the string can be a useful way of encouraging impulsion when holding it doubled up in one hand and swinging it gently from side-to-side.

Duct Tape

A bit of duct tape strategically placed on your training tools can help take the guesswork out of correct hand position.

Place a strip of duct tape around each rein, about 18 inches to two feet from the bit. This will serve as a visual aid for where to put your hand for various riding cues.

❋ *Cecelia*

"When I saw Clinton coming at us with the duct tape, I thought 'surely he won't put that on my expensive leather reins!' That's exactly what he did. I have to admit, it was very helpful to use as a visual aid—one less thing I had to think about. When I no longer needed the reference point, the tape eventually came off."

Spurs

Spurs can be a valuable training aid. They are not to be used as punishment. They simply reinforce leg pressure, making it easier for the horse to interpret a cue.

I prefer spurs with blunt rowels. When gently rolled along the horse's body, the rowels provide a clear, consistent cue. Blunt-end spurs can also be effective with a very sensitive horse.

Spurs should fit well and remain snugly in place on your heel during use. Do not use spurs if you use your lower leg to grab onto the horse for balance.

Boots and Wraps

Using protective leg boots on a horse when training him will help minimize strains and soreness. Be sure to keep your horse's legs and boots clean.

Dressage Whip

A dressage whip can be an effective tool for impulsion when riding. Use the whip gently and rhythmically behind your leg to reinforce your cues. Remember, because they are so thin and flexible, dressage whips can direct a great deal of pressure toward the horse. The purpose of the whip is to reinforce a cue.

7.3

Leg position is important when using spurs as training aids.

8

BEFORE YOU RIDE

From the Ground Up

I highly recommend that you master the *Essential Groundwork Exercises* (p. 49) before beginning *Essential Exercises Under Saddle* (p. 135).

Here's why:

Establishing and maintaining your *Hula Hoop* of personal space shows the horse that he must respect you.

Because of the *Desensitizing Exercises*, your horse realizes that he can trust you. He has learned to use the *thinking* side of his brain, rather than simply *reacting* to a new situation. These exercises help ensure that the horse isn't a fearful bundle of nerves. The more relaxed your horse is, the more relaxed you can be.

Disengaging the Hindquarters, Backing, and *Yielding the Forequarters* give you control over various parts of the horse's body. These three "primary exercises" provide the foundation for most advanced riding maneuvers. Rollbacks, spins, lead changes, half-passes, extension,

collection, pirouettes, piaffe, passage, and more, all build on the basic movements of these three exercises.

As an added bonus, disengaging the hindquarters while under saddle will become your foolproof emergency brake.

Groundwork results in a horse that is more supple and respectful. He learns how to move different areas of his body in response to specific cues from you. Groundwork also allows most major issues of disrespect to surface and be dealt with before moving on to work under saddle.

Lungeing and *Circle Driving* exercises assure that the horse pays attention to you, even when his feet are moving.

Sending and *Leading Beside* exercises teach your horse to be responsible for his own actions. Before you get in the saddle, your horse should have learned some control over the *reacting* part of his brain.

8.1
Groundwork prepares a horse to perform under saddle. It can make riding enjoyable for both horse and rider.

In addition, by the time you have done the ground exercises, both you and your horse will have built a rapport. You will have learned a way of communicating more effectively. You will have firmly established yourself as someone worthy of your horse's respect and attention.

Saddling

Use saddling time as learning time. You may want to do a few Desensitizing Exercises with the saddle if the horse has a tendency to be flighty. If the horse must be tied because he moves sideways to avoid the saddle, now is the time to break the habit.

Saddle the horse in the open. Have a rope halter and 14-foot lead rope on him, but hold the rope loosely, with quite a bit of slack in it.

The horse should stand quietly while you tack him up.

If he shows an interest, let him smell the saddle and pad. Show the equipment to him from both sides.

When saddling, stand at a 45-degree angle to the horse's shoulder, facing his rear. If the horse flinches or jumps when you throw the saddle pad up on his back, treat the episode as a desensitizing exercise. Repeat throwing the saddle pad with rhythm until the horse stands quietly. Do the same sort of thing with the saddle. Be especially aware of letting the horse see you with the saddle on his right side.

Keep your horse's comfort in mind. Lift the saddle pad up off the withers. This creates a "pocket" for airflow and promotes circula-

8.4

Groundwork enables you to clearly communicate with your horse under saddle.

tion. Adjust your girth or cinches snugly, but gradually. If wrinkles of skin appear between the girth and the horse's side, lift his front legs one at a time and stretch them out in front of him to minimize the possibility of girth galls.

If the horse dances during saddling, practice some desensitizing techniques. You may also want to some energetic Backing exercises or Disengage the Hindquarters to assure that he is listening to you.

Check that your saddle fits your horse properly. The tree should be strong and wide enough to avoid pinching his shoulders when he is in full stride. Keep your leather clean, well-oiled, and in good condition. Clean girths and saddle pads regularly.

Bridling

Many people prefer to leave the halter on under the bridle when training. Use your judg-

ment. If you take the halter off the horse's head, place it around his neck before bridling. This allows you to retain some control. If necessary, you can pull on the halter to get both eyes focused on you.

For easy bridling, stand on the horse's left. Hold the headstall in your right hand, resting your hand between the horse's ears. Hold the bit against your left palm. Your left hand guides the bit into the horse's mouth. If the horse doesn't willingly open his mouth for the bit, wiggle your left thumb inside and against the roof of the mouth. When the horse accepts the bit, lift the headstall over the ears.

Make sure that your bridle is properly adjusted. The throatlatch should be tight enough that the bridle cannot slip over the horse's ears if he shakes his head. It should be loose enough that the horse can bend at the poll without cutting off his air supply.

Impulsion Cues and Considerations

SQUEEZE, CLUCK, SPANK

To train your horse to respond to a subtle cue for forward impulsion, you should always begin with that cue. Give the horse a chance to associate the cue with moving forward.

As with every series of cues you have taught your horse to this point, begin softly. A gentle squeeze of your legs on the horse's sides is sufficient. The squeeze *asks* the horse to move forward.

If the horse doesn't move forward at the gait and speed you want, continue gently squeezing. Add one or two verbal "clucks" as well. The clucks *tell* the horse to move forward.

If the horse still refuses to move, increase the pressure. Maintain the gentle squeeze. Cluck a time or two. Then "spank" from side-to-side (fig. 8.5).

Your "spanker" can be either the free end of the mecate reins or the string, doubled up and slipped over one wrist, with the tail ends hanging loose. Spanking *motivates* the horse to move forward.

At any time in the process, when the horse moves forward at the desired gait, immediately release the pressure from all cues. The horse should learn to maintain the gait you ask for without constant nagging.

WHAT IF YOU STILL DON'T GO?

Avoid the temptation, especially on a lazy horse, to kick him to make him go forward. Kicking acts like large-scale desensitizing. Eventually, you have to kick all the time in order to get the horse to respond.

If you spank and the horse doesn't go the speed you want, keep spanking with rhythm until he does. If you stop spanking before he does the right thing, you teach him not to listen to you.

When spanking, as with everything, begin gently. The goal is not to frighten or shock the horse into bolting forward and dumping you. The purpose is to back up the earlier leg (squeeze) and voice (cluck) cues.

Your horse may kick out when you first spank with the mecate rope or string. This is his way of saying "get lost." Bend his head around and keep spanking from side-to-side. Move him with high energy in a small circle to correct him for kicking, then resume the original exercise.

How long should you ride?

Most people quit far too soon when it comes to concentrating their energy on riding exercises. Remember: long rides, wet saddle blankets, and concentrated training. Stimulate your horse mentally and physically and his progress will amaze you.

When teaching anything that asks for forward impulsion, be prepared to ride at a particular gait for 10 to 15 minutes at a time until the horse relaxes, understands what you expect of him, learns to balance himself, and finds his rhythm.

In my opinion, the enjoyment of riding is not about preferring one discipline—English or Western—over another. It is about horsemanship.

I try not to be a clock-watcher when I ride. I enjoy every minute spent on a respectful, willing horse. It doesn't matter what breed the horse is or how far his training has advanced. If the horse has been taught to trust his rider and try what his rider asks, I like to think that he enjoys every minute of the experience as well.

9

ESSENTIAL EXERCISES
UNDER SADDLE

Flexing to the Bridle

Goal

To lightly pick up on one rein and have the horse immediately yield to the pressure, turn his head, and touch the stirrup with his nose.

Why Do It?

When a horse flexes, he turns his head and neck to one side or the other, yielding to pressure. Teaching the horse to flex laterally (from side-to-side) lays the foundation for later teaching vertical (up-and-down) flexion.

A horse that readily flexes is light on the bit and responsive to bridle cues. His direction and impulsion are easily controlled. His neck and jaw are soft and pliable.

Flexing lays the groundwork for many of the exercises in this book. If your horse is light and soft to one rein, either from the ground or under saddle, it makes a tremendous differ-

ence in your control. It also greatly increases your safety. When you are thirty miles from home, the last thing you want is to fall or get bucked off. Every horse I train learns to flex. It has saved me from walking for miles more times than I care to count.

Stage One—Flexing from the Ground

Teaching Steps

1. With the horse bridled and saddled, stand by the flank with your belly button facing him. Put the reins over the horse's head so they hang loosely and rest on his neck in front of the withers. The horse must be able to turn his head freely from side to side without coming into contact with the outside rein.

IMPORTANT
NOTE
·········
Before attempting this exercise with a bridle, you and your horse should have mastered **Flexing to the Halter** *(p. 91).*

9.1

Flexing to the Bridle helps the horse to be light and responsive.

2. "Hug" the top of the horse's hindquarters with the arm closest to the tail. With the hand closest to the horse's head, grasp the inside rein about two feet from the bit.

3. Pull the rein hand to the seat of the saddle. Maintain the pressure and stay with the horse if he moves his feet.

4. When the horse yields to the pressure and touches his belly, instantly drop the rein out of your hand.

5. Flex several times on both sides before mounting.

Common Handler Mistakes

• Standing too far forward. Standing too close to the horse's shoulder blocks him. Allow him enough space to bend his neck around.

• Pulling the rein over the horse's back or up in the air. Keep your rein hand on the same side of the horse's spine as you are. "Glue" your rein hand to the saddle.

• Releasing too slowly when the horse gives. Even if your horse gives well to halter pressure, remember that the bridle is a new situation. Don't expect your horse to immediately understand what you want and flex as lightly as he does in the halter. You must reward the slightest try at first.

• Not letting the horse rest between flexes. Let the horse's head and neck straighten out completely for at least four or five seconds before pulling on the rein for another flex.

• Jerking on the rein. Jerking on the horse's mouth will not create a light, responsive animal. Be patient and wait for the horse to yield to the pressure you create.

Common Horse Problems

• Walking in circles. Maintain your posi-

tion. Stay with the horse and wait until he stops his feet and softens to the bit.

• Nibbling on the stirrup or smelling you. At first, ignore the behavior. The horse is just investigating. Some horses will do this if you hold the rein too long without releasing when they give.

• Falsely giving. If your horse bends his nose around, but doesn't create any slack in the rein, don't release the pressure. Keep holding the rein until he truly yields, creating some slack in the rein.

Troubleshooting

• If your horse doesn't seem to understand what you are asking of him, be sure that you are not pulling too hard on the reins. Also, be sure that you are releasing immediately to reward the slightest try.

Tips for Success

• Before doing any flexing with a bit, be sure that your horse flexes well with the halter.

✳ *Cecelia*

"Don't change tactics because of a change in equipment. When Smacks was saddled, I started pulling the rein to the top of the withers instead of pulling to where I would have without the saddle. I had to be consistent with my cues, regardless of what he was wearing."

✳ *Paula*

"I needed to change bits. I originally used a tom thumb and Clinton had us use a snaffle for these riding exercises. I knew Fancy was responding to a specific cue rather than to the leverage of a bit shank."

Stage Two—Flexing Under Saddle

Teaching Steps

1. After mounting, hold the middle of the reins with one hand. Anchor that hand on the horn or pommel of the saddle, with no contact or pressure on the horse's mouth.
2. Slide the other hand halfway down one rein. Holding the rein firmly, pull your hand to your hip and keep it there, until the horse stands quietly and softens his neck.
3. When the horse creates slack in the rein and touches your stirrup, drop the rein. Repeat the exercise, alternating from side-to-side, for three to five minutes on each side (figs. 9.2 A & B).

Common Rider Mistakes

• Not sliding your hand down far enough on the flexing rein. If your cueing rein isn't short, your horse won't flex around far enough (fig. 9.3).

• Pulling the horse's head all the way around or jerking the reins. As in *Stage One*, give your horse the opportunity to get the exercise right. Only pull three-quarters of the way around. Let him give the rest of the way.

• Not releasing when the horse gives. The faster you release the rein, the faster the horse will understand that he did the right thing.

• Taking slack out of the outside rein. If the outside rein is tight, your horse will have difficulty flexing. The looser the outside rein, the quicker the horse will learn.

• Gripping with your legs. Squeezing with your legs during this exercise will encourage the horse to walk in a circle. Keep your legs relaxed. Don't give your horse a reason to move his feet.

Common Horse Problems

• Spinning in circles. Keep the hand with the cueing rein on your hip. Wait until the horse's feet stop and his head and neck soften.

• Leaning on the bit. Be patient and wait. If your cueing hand gets tired, hook your thumb in a pocket to keep the correct position.

• Lifting his head in the air or pushing his nose down low. Ignore these little quirks and keep flexing. The more you do, the more the horse will understand what is expected of him, and the bad behavior will stop.

Troubleshooting

• When first asked to flex, most horses will nibble on your foot or your stirrup as they try to figure out what you want. If the problem persists for more than a couple of weeks, or if the horse becomes more aggressive, lightly kick him on the nose with your foot. Make the horse understand that biting is not a game.

Tips for Success

• I encourage riders to flex their horses and rub their faces. Let the horse know you are on top of him. This is especially effective for hot, nervous horses and young colts.

❋ *Cecelia*

"Remember to keep the free hand in the horse's mane or on the pommel of the saddle. The hand that is not pulling the flexing rein needs to be anchored on something.

"Just as when flexing to the halter, don't pull the head all the way around. Only pull three-quarters of the way. That last little bit is the horse's job."

When cueing, keep constant tension on the rein. Release immediately when the horse gives.

*Slide your hand
about halfway down
the cueing rein.*

✳ *Paula*

"Fancy understood this so quickly. I know that is because of all the work we did Flexing to the Halter.

"As soon as we mounted, Clinton had us flex our horses for five minutes straight. Fancy got so light and responsive. It made a huge difference when we began riding—she had already been reminded about her steering and was nicely limbered up for work."

One-Rein Stop

Goal

To have the horse stop at any gait and soften when you pick up on one rein.

Why Do It?

This exercise serves as your "emergency brake." If you teach your horse to immediately stop and soften every time you pick up on one rein, you have a better chance of gaining control if your horse suddenly spooks or takes off. It also teaches the horse to be responsible for maintaining the exact speed you ask for.

I learned the value of this exercise while working with young horses in Australia. Often, while riding through the brush, a kangaroo would suddenly jump out and startle the horses. They would be frightened and try to bolt. A *One-Rein Stop* enabled the rider to quickly get the situation under control. Pulling back on both reins, on the other hand, allowed the horse to brace his neck against the pressure and run for some distance before he could be stopped, increasing the potential for injuring himself or his rider.

Teaching Steps

1. Release all pressure on the reins. Ask the horse to go forward at a walk for 15 to 20 feet. *Do not steer.*

2. To stop, slide one hand down a rein to the

duct tape and pull it to your hip, as you did in *Flexing Under Saddle* (p. 137). Keep your other hand on the middle of the reins.

3. Wait until the horse completely stops his feet, gives to the rein pressure, and touches your boot or stirrup with his nose. When the horse flexes, immediately open the hand on your hip and release the rein.

4. Repeat the exercise, alternating which rein you use for stopping. Continue this exercise at the walk until the horse maintains a consistent, even walk without slowing or speeding up.

5. When the horse understands the exercise at the walk, do it at a trot. Then do it at a canter. Do not ask the horse to move to a faster gait until he has mastered the slower ones.

Common Rider Mistakes

• Not sliding the hand down far enough on the rein. Use duct tape for a visual aid, as explained in *Riding Tools* (p. 123).

• Releasing the rein too soon. The horse must do two things before you release the rein: stop moving his feet and soften to the bit. If you release while he is still moving, he won't understand that he should stop. If you release before the horse softens and yields to the pressure, he may get in the habit of pulling against you when you pick up the rein.

• Steering. Don't. It is easiest for your horse to learn one thing at a time. Let him go wherever he wants on a loose rein until you do a One-Rein Stop.

• Clutching at the reins. If you are afraid your horse will spook, take off, or jump out from under you, do a lot of One-Rein Stops. Don't let him build up too much speed or momentum. Walk a few strides, then stop. Walk a few more strides, then stop again. If you think your horse might try something, stop him, but only use one rein to do it. Grabbing at the reins in fear only teaches the horse that you are afraid of him and it gives him something to brace against.

• Speeding up too soon. Don't move up to the next gait until the slower ones are very good. It should go without saying that if the horse is trying to take off at the trot, don't canter.

• Jerking on the rein to stop. Don't yank the horse's head around—especially if he is cantering. You could cause the horse to fall. Grab the rein calmly and pull to your hip in a fluid motion.

• Letting the horse go too far. If the horse is allowed to go too far, he may start to build speed and forget about listening to you. The hotter and more nervous a horse is, the less distance you should go between stops.

• Grabbing with your legs. Squeeze to get the horse moving. But once he is going forward, remove the pressure. Remember to keep leg pressure off of him when doing the One-Rein Stop.

Common Horse Problems:

• Preferring one spot of the arena. If your horse wants to "stick" at a certain spot, such as the in-gate or near another horse, let him. Let him go where he wants. As soon as he stops moving his feet, squeeze, cluck, spank, and get the feet moving. Ask the horse to stop somewhere else. Eventually he will realize that he has to work—even at his favorite place.

• Anticipating moving after stopping. If the horse tries to walk off before you ask him to, spend some time Flexing Under Saddle. Continue flexing from side-to-side until your horse stands quietly and waits for your cue. Let him rest a few moments. Then ask him to move off. Make sure it is *your* idea to move forward.

• Going too fast. If your horse speeds up, do the One-Rein Stop. Don't let him go so many strides that he gets out of control. Be sure to maintain a loose rein. Dare your horse to make a mistake—then correct him when he does.

• Laziness. Be sure that your impulsion cues are clear and consistent. Give the horse an incentive to want to go forward.

Troubleshooting

• When moving to a canter, after the horse has mastered this exercise at a walk and a trot, canter no more than five strides before doing a One-Rein Stop. Don't give the horse the opportunity to run away with you. The more One-Rein Stops you do at the canter, the more you improve your "emergency brake."

• If the horse wants to go fast all the time, make sure your reins are loose and you aren't putting too much pressure on him. When he goes the right speed, immediately remove any pressure. The horse will soon figure out that when you ask him to move, he doesn't have to go fast.

Tips for Success

• If you find that one side is stiffer than the other, flex the horse to a stop on the stiff side more often. Working both sides will make your horse more balanced, as well.

• Spend at least 10 minutes doing One-Rein Stops at each gait before moving on.

• Regardless of whether you ride English or Western, post at the trot for this exercise. This helps keep you in rhythm with your horse and improves your balance. Sit three strides before doing the One-Rein Stop. This helps the horse start to associate your weight shifting back with stopping.

✳ *Cecelia*

"At first, Smacks wanted to sling his head around. He had developed the habit because he had learned that he could rip the reins out of my hands. But riding on a loose rein made it a moot point. Clinton told me to ignore the head flinging and eventually it would stop. He was right.

"I needed to be reminded not to let go of the flexing rein when Smacks yielded, if his feet hadn't stopped moving yet. Both the stop *and* the yield are important.

"Smacks wanted to stop on his own near Fancy. Clinton told me not to let him. I kept his feet moving. Smacks learned that being around Fancy wouldn't save him from working.

"I threw all my cues together a little too fast, at first. I got nervous and grabbed Smacks' mouth. I had to calm down and cue a little more smoothly to give him a chance to respond. As we did the One-Rein Stops—millions of them—he got more and more relaxed. It was wonderful. As he relaxed, so did I.

"After working on this lesson, Smacks started cantering and then slowed by himself. He anticipated me stopping. Soon, he wasn't trying to canter so fast because he knew we were going to stop soon."

✳ *Paula*

"I'll admit, I was afraid. I worried, 'What if I don't tell her to go and she does?' But the One-Rein Stop works. Fancy can't ignore it. She has to listen to me.

"To get Fancy to move, I was clucking at her like a chicken, nagging her. Clinton reminded me to squeeze with my legs, cluck a bit, and then follow up with a spank. Clucking like a mother hen just teaches her to ignore my voice.

"I wasn't confident about staying on. I either clutched at her or let her trot off too far before stopping. It took a little bit to get over my fear before I could do the exercise well. Clinton kept stressing that we were only to go a few strides before doing the One-Rein Stop. He didn't want us to get out of control. Soon, I realized that I really could stop her if I needed to. That made a huge difference in my confidence!"

Cruising

9.6

Cruising helps your horse take responsibility for his gait and speed—allowing you just to ride.

Goal

To have your horse move off promptly at a trot or canter and maintain the desired gait until asked to change.

Why Do It?

Cruising teaches the horse to take responsibility for his gait and speed while ignoring movements from his rider that are not specific cues.

I do a lot of Cruising when starting young colts. When training horses, my main priorities are a good "gas pedal" and "brake" (the *One-Rein Stop*). But, teaching the horse how to move forward and how to steer at the same time can be confusing. If you let the horse cruise, without fighting over direction, he quickly gains confidence at all three gaits. Cruising also teaches the horse that when you set a certain pace, he should maintain that pace.

An added value of the exercise is that it teaches the rider to have an independent seat. The rider learns to stay with the horse without grabbing with the legs or hanging on the reins.

9.7

Move around in the saddle. Accustom the horse to seeing you there.

Many riders want to keep contact with the horse's mouth. If you ride with constant contact for several hours at a stretch, the horse will soon become hard in the mouth and generally resistant. Ride regularly on a loose rein, expecting the horse to be responsible for his gait and speed. Then, when you do pick up contact with the horse's mouth, the cue is specific, and the horse will pay closer attention to it.

Teaching Steps

1. Hold the middle of the reins and the pommel or horn of the saddle with one hand. The reins should hang loosely and make no contact with the bit. Hold the string or the end of the mecate with your other hand.

2. Cue the horse for forward impulsion until he trots. Post at the trot. Do not try to influence the horse's direction. *Do not steer.* If the horse walks or stops, immediately squeeze, cluck, and spank for forward impulsion. If the horse canters, do a One-Rein Stop, then trot again.

3. When your horse trots calmly, move all around in the saddle. Rub (do not slap) the horse's neck, withers, and hindquarters. Slap your hand on your leg or on the saddle in rhythm with the horse's stride. Wave your arms back and forth. Get the horse used to seeing you moving up on top of him (fig. 9.7). Rely on your One-Rein Stop if the horse breaks into a canter.

IMPORTANT NOTE
• • • • • • • •

This exercise works best in a large arena or field. Do not teach **Cruising** *on or near a road. Before learning this exercise, you and your horse should have mastered the* **One-Rein Stop** *(see p. 140). Review the* **Impulsion Cues** *(see p. 133).*

4. Trot for at least 15 minutes. Do a One-Rein Stop. Rub the horse. Allow him to stand quietly while you practice *Flexing Under Saddle* (see p. 137) for several minutes. Repeat Cruising at the trot for at least another 10 minutes.

5. When you and your horse have mastered this exercise at the trot, do it at a canter.

Common Rider Mistakes

• Trying to steer. This exercise is as much for the rider as it is for the horse. Hold on to the mane or the saddle and just *ride*.

• Sitting the trot. Whether you ride English or Western, post when doing this exercise at the trot. Posting helps keep you in rhythm with your horse.

• Stopping too soon. Many people want to quit after a minute or two. Do not quit until your horse is completely relaxed, well-balanced, and consistent.

• Correcting the horse too soon. Wait until the horse makes a mistake before correcting him. Otherwise, he will never learn to maintain the gait you ask for on his own.

• Worrying about diagonals and leads. Instead of concerning yourself with diagonals and leads, concentrate on riding in rhythm with the horse.

Common Horse Problems

• Going too fast. As long as the horse maintains the gait you have cued for, don't worry about his speed, at this point. As soon as the horse takes one stride of a faster gait, do a One-Rein Stop. Shut off the gas. Don't give him the opportunity to run away with you. If the horse continually breaks into a faster gait, review the One-Rein Stop before continuing this exercise.

• Breaking into a trot from a canter. Cue for forward impulsion until the horse canters again. Don't correct the horse until he makes a mistake.

• Wanting to stay by other horses in the area. Keep your horse's feet moving in the desired gait. Pretend that yours is the only horse in the arena. Ignore the other horses as much as possible. Resist the temptation to pull your horse away from the others. It will only interrupt the exercise and increase his desire to be with his friends. When he realizes he still has to work—even near his buddies—they will no longer seem so attractive.

Troubleshooting

• At first, your horse will probably zigzag all over the arena. Don't try to guess what direction he will go. Relax, and keep your seat in the saddle. If necessary, use the hand with the "spanker" to hold on to the cantle of the saddle.

Tips for Success

• Canter your horse a lot. Make this part of your regular routine. Often, horses want to go fast when cantering because they have never practiced the gait enough to do it slowly.

• Always end this exercise at a relaxed trot. That way, the last thing the horse remembers is being relaxed and moving forward on a loose rein.

✸ *Cecelia*

"I really had to work on myself to not clutch at my horse. I just had to sit back, relax, and let him find his stride and be accountable for himself.

"I had a tendency to want to correct

Post when trotting, but don't concern yourself with diagonals. Focus on balance and rhythm.

Smacks before he made the mistake. I could feel him speeding up at the trot and knew he was going to break into a canter. Clinton told me to wait until he actually cantered before I corrected him.

"I was afraid at first—I knew what acrobatics Smacks was capable of. But the One-Rein Stop works wonders.

"The motor skills are very cumbersome in the beginning. At first, the 'stop' and 'go' cues

9.9

To keep your seat when cantering, you may prefer to hold the cantle.

aren't very fluid. It takes a sustained time to learn this. One thing Clinton said that I appreciated is 'you'll figure it out.' You don't have to be picture perfect in order to be effective."

✳ Paula

"Fancy cut left and right and changed directions a lot at first. Balance is so impor-

tant. If you don't have good balance, you will fall off. I liked that Clinton told me I could hold onto the back of my saddle. It helped me to feel more secure. I couldn't use my hands to hold the reins and steer anyway.

"A couple of times Fancy sped up into a canter and I thought, 'She's taking off!' I know it wasn't terribly fast, but it felt fast to me, and

I was a little scared. The One-Rein Stop we had practiced did the trick. That was all I needed to calm myself down, regroup, and trot again.

"After the first session (where we worked at a trot for over half an hour), my legs were so tired. I wasn't used to posting and felt like I was flopping all over the place. It took a while for me to feel comfortable posting.

"The duct tape on the reins was very helpful. I was so worried about Fancy possibly taking off and cantering or bucking. The duct tape took away one of the variables. I didn't have to think about where to put my hand on the reins when I went to stop. It was one less thing to worry about.

"I am loving this! I am finally enjoying my horse. In my opinion, every horse owner needs this. I don't care if you have ridden for a hundred years or if you have just started, you can benefit from these exercises."

And, after a few Cruising rides:

❋ *Cecelia*

"I wanted to kick a little or grab with my legs if Smacks ignored the squeezing cues. Clinton reminded me that was what the spank was for. I liked that—it kept my leg cues light and still ensured that Smacks stayed responsive.

"Clinton said that riding a horse like Smacks with constant contact made him feel lost if the contact wasn't there. This horse had *never* been ridden on a loose rein—especially at the canter. I didn't trust him, so he had never learned to be trustworthy.

"Clinton also had me move a lot, rubbing Smacks all over his neck and everywhere I could reach. The more I move on him while

we are cantering, the more confident I act, and the more he relaxes.

"Making these exercises part of the everyday training routine is so important. The difference in my horse after a few short days is astounding. I'm a believer!"

❋ *Paula*

"I felt so much more secure about cantering after Cruising for thirty minutes. We rested for fifteen minutes to give Fancy 'time to think about things.' Then we cantered again for another half hour. Cantering is actually getting to be enjoyable now.

"Amazingly, I wasn't too afraid of her bucking. What Clinton says is true: if Fancy is going forward, she can't do much more than kick up a little behind her. I know now to spank her forward through any bucking fit she might think of pitching. But she never even thought of kicking up. We had done so much groundwork, and her level of respect for me was so high, she wasn't interested in using the energy to pick a fight with me.

"Clinton had to tell me to loosen up and move all over while we rode. I was riding stiffly, trying not to make any sudden move that might frighten my horse. When I started purposely moving around, rubbing her neck, patting behind the saddle, patting my leg, and not being so much like a statue, I got a lot more relaxed and more confident. I also started expecting more from her.

"I learned to stop worrying about every little thing that could go wrong. I loosened up and relaxed and started enjoying myself so much more."

Follow the Fence

Follow the Fence *teaches the horse to be responsible for maintaining direction.*

Goal

To have the horse trot or canter along the fence line without any "steering" required from the rider.

Why Do It?

Follow the Fence builds on what the horse learned in *Cruising* (p. 144). In addition to making the horse responsible for maintaining a desired gait, it makes him responsible for going in a particular direction.

Some horses wiggle and weave all over the place. I want my horse to learn to travel straight without needing constant redirection. The fence is a useful tool.

I spent many hours following fences in Australia. Checking a 15,000 acre pasture for broken fences involves a lot of trotting in a straight line.

Mastering this exercise frees you to ride without micro-managing every little thing your horse does. It also allows your horse to move more freely, trusting that you will let him know when you want him to change speed or direction.

Teaching Steps

1. Ask your horse to trot around the arena. Hold the middle of the reins with your inside hand. Anchor your rein hand in the horse's mane or on the saddle.

2. Keep the horse trotting next to the fence. Every time your horse comes more than four feet away from the fence, slide your free hand down the outside rein, point to the fence, and put pressure on the rein. Drop the rein when the horse is close to the fence again (figs. 9.11 A–C).

3. Trot in one direction for 10 to 15 minutes or as long as it takes for the horse to understand the lesson. Post while trotting. When the horse understands the lesson, stop in a corner or in an area that he likes the least. Rest for 5 to 10 minutes. Change directions and repeat the exercise.

4. When the horse can Follow the Fence well at a trot, do the exercise at a canter.

Common Rider Mistakes

- Neck reining. This exercise is all about teaching the horse to follow his nose and make the right decisions. Pull left to go left; pull right to go right.

- Releasing the cueing rein too soon. Hold the outside rein until the horse is back on the fence. If you drop the rein and reward him before he gets all the way there, he will learn to cheat on you and not move his feet close to the fence.

- Pulling on the reins to regulate speed. This exercise must be done on a loose rein. Remember, it is the horse's responsibility to maintain gait and direction. If he breaks to a faster gait, correct him with one rein, pulling it toward the fence until his feet slow down. Continue the exercise. *Do not pull back on both reins.* This will only encourage the horse to pull against you, which is the opposite of the light responsiveness that you want.

- Quitting too soon. Trot or canter your horse until you feel him slowing down, wanting to stop, then keep going for another few minutes. This helps make the horse more responsive when you *do* ask him to stop. It also teaches him to conserve his energy, use his body more effectively, and appreciate the slow, quiet exercises.

- Changing directions without resting. Once the horse understands the exercise in one direction, let him rest for a few minutes before going the other way. Don't mix directions at first. Work on only one side of his brain at a time.

- Pulling the rein to the hip. Instead of cueing the horse to flex his neck, point toward the fence. Encourage him to follow your hand and rein.

Common Horse Problems

• Spooking at objects along the arena. Tip the horse's nose toward the spooky object and continue the exercise.

• Veering off of the fence. Allow the horse to make the mistake of coming at least four feet off the rail before guiding him back toward the fence. You may also apply light pressure with your inside leg at the same time as your hand cue. Some horses require quite a bit of guiding back to the fence at first. Be patient and consistent.

• Cutting corners. Consider this as coming off the fence. Use your outside rein to guide the horse as far into the corner as possible, then drop the rein.

9.11 A–C

Allow the horse to commit the mistake and come off the rail. Steer him back to the fence. Release the rein and let the horse be responsible for himself.

• Trying to run you into the fence. Pull the outside rein and bump the horse's nose into the fence every time he tries to run your leg too close to the rail.

• Cantering on the wrong lead. At first, don't worry about leads. At the very least, can-tering on the wrong lead will improve your horse's balance. Before long, your horse should learn which lead is most comfortable in a given direction.

• Breaking gait. If your horse consistently breaks gait, review Cruising (p. 144), or the

One-Rein Stop (p. 140). He may not be ready for this exercise yet.

Troubleshooting

• If you have consistent trouble getting your horse to stay by the fence, near a gate, or in a corner, go to that spot to let him rest before changing directions.

Tips for Success

• You should be able to reach out and touch the fence at any time while doing this exercise.

• Do not canter this exercise until you and your horse have mastered it at the trot. The faster you go, the more obvious any resistance becomes.

✷ *Cecelia*

"I had to be reminded to pick up more softly and not grab at the rein I used for cueing.

"Right after we did this lesson, Clinton caught me using both reins to stop. It is so easy to revert to old habits. I have to retrain myself as much as the horse.

"Smacks has always cut corners. I was surprised at how quickly he learned to be responsible for himself. All I had to do was correct him when he got it wrong. Soon he was navigating deep into the corners. Even better—he was balanced and bent the right way!

"At this point, I have to remember not to criticize Smacks for dropping to a trot when I relax. Since he still has a lot of get up and go, when he voluntarily slows down, my job is not to make him feel uncomfortable about it. I just calmly ask for the canter again and he willingly gives it to me.

"Now, when I relax, he relaxes. He is more in tune to my body language. Thanks to this and to Cruising, we have a new gear: a nice, slow, ratable lope!"

✷ *Paula*

"Fancy had some problems with this exercise at first. She kept wanting to stop and wasn't really getting the forward motion she needed. Clinton pointed out that this is what happens when you start steering without a good gas pedal. I had to go back and do more Cruising until she loosened up her feet again.

"Pointing with my hand in the direction where I wanted to go really helped. Clinton told me not to drop the rein just because the horse's head bent toward the fence. I needed to cue until her body followed her head and she got to the fence.

"Clinton also reminded me to take my hand off the saddle horn and work on my own balance when Fancy was moving nice and slow.

"After the very first time we did this exercise, the horses started to stay on the fence much better. By the second day, if they started to drift, they usually corrected themselves."

Bending

Goal

To have the horse walk forward and around in a small circle, yielding around your leg, and softening to rein pressure.

Why Do It?

Bending builds on the *Flexing* exercises. In addition to flexing laterally, the horse also learns to move his feet in a controlled manner.

Bending is helpful if your horse is nervous or uptight. It helps him pay attention to you and concentrate on something other than spooking.

If your horse is very stiff, Bending will be difficult for him at first, and he will be reluctant to do so. Through practice, however, he will grow more and more comfortable with the exercise.

Nothing is more effective for getting the horse soft and supple from his nose all the way to his tail. When your horse is supple throughout the length of his body, anything you want him to do—whether it is cutting, reining, contesting, dressage, hunting, or jumping—will be possible.

When I was a kid in Australia, I had a horse that I used for playing polocrosse. He was hot, nervous and didn't want to stop. He would throw his head in the air constantly. My friend Gordon McKinlay told me that in order to fix my horse's problems, I should do nothing but *One-Rein Stops* and bending exercises for a whole week.

I took his advice. At the end of the week, I cantered the horse along, picked up on the reins and said, "Whoa." My horse slid to a stop, backed up, and tucked his nose in so fast, I nearly fell off in shock. That incident proved to me that lateral flexion is the key to vertical flexion.

Teaching Steps

1. Ask the horse to walk forward on a loose rein. Hold the middle of the reins with one hand. Anchor your hand in the horse's mane or on the saddle.
2. Slide your free hand down one rein. Pull the rein to your hip (fig. 9.13). At the same time, add pressure with the leg on the same side (the inside), encouraging your horse to continue moving. If the horse stops walking, roll your spur up his side, or spank him with rhythm until his feet move.
3. When the horse walks forward in a circle and softens to the bit, immediately straighten your inside elbow and drop your inside hand to your knee. Do not drop the rein out of your hand. At the same time, release all leg pressure.
4. When the horse straightens his head and neck, bring your rein hand back to your hip and apply your inside leg again.
5. Every time the horse softens to the bit while walking, drop your rein hand to your knee and release all leg pressure. Eventually, he will bend and continue walking without pressure on the rein or from your inside leg.
6. Bend your horse in three or four circles. When the horse responds well, let him walk straight for at least 10 feet, then bend him the other way.
7. When the horse has mastered bending at the walk, do transitions. Trot off in any direction. Bend the horse to a walk. After three or four bending circles, trot straight off, and repeat the exercise. When the horse has mastered the exercise at the trot, practice it at a canter.

Common Handler Mistakes

• Not using the leg and rein cues together. If you don't use your inside leg, the horse will walk around with a stiff body instead of arcing around a circle. If you don't release your leg cue when you release the rein, the horse will learn to ignore it and lean against it.

Anchor your cueing hand on your hip for consistency. Be sure to keep slack in the outside rein.

• Releasing late. Releasing the rein pressure as soon as your horse "gives" will reward him. If you don't release on time, the horse will begin to pull against pressure rather than yield to it.

• Letting the forward motion stop. Keep the horse's feet moving by rolling your spur or spanking behind your legs with the mecate. Even when you stop circling and go straight forward, keep his feet moving (fig. 9.14).

• Circling too long. Do three or four circles before letting the horse walk straight. If you circle too long, he may get frustrated and lock up on you—especially in the beginning.

• Using your outside leg. Don't. Your inside leg creates the bend and encourages forward motion. Only use your outside leg when the horse's shoulders don't follow his nose.

Essential Exercises Under Saddle

Taking your foot out of the stirrup may help you give a more consistent cue.

Common Horse Problems

• Not moving forward. If the horse resists moving forward in the circle, use less rein pressure. Spank behind your leg with the end of the mecate or with the string. In the beginning, you may need to sacrifice some of the bend to get the forward motion.

• Tipping or shaking the head to the side.

Once the horse softens and understands the exercise, this behavior will stop.

• Trotting in a circle. If your horse trots in response to your leg or spur, be sure you aren't using your leg too aggressively. Gently hold the pressure against his side until he walks. If you release the cue when he trots, you will teach him that running makes the pressure go away.

Troubleshooting

- If the horse doesn't want to walk forward, even if you aren't asking for a lot of bend, over exaggerate the concept of forward motion. Trot the horse in a small circle every time he doesn't want to go forward. Review *Cruising* (p. 144).

Tips for Success

- If you have trouble knowing when to release the rein and leg pressure, watch the horse's nose. Every time his nose comes toward your toe, release the pressure.
- Spurs can help lazy or dull horses master this exercise faster. However, if you need your lower legs for balance, don't wear spurs. Instead, use the dressage whip or the end of the mecate for more forward movement.

❋ *Cecelia*

"I learned to spank behind my leg, rather than in front of it, to get the forward motion. I had a tendency to spank all the time—nagging at my horse. Clinton reminded me to spank only when Smacks loses his impulsion. If he is moving, I leave him alone.

"At some times, I was in too much of a hurry to grab at the rein and pick up on his mouth. I was trying too much, pulling on him too quickly and too hard. I needed to get more fluid and smooth with my cues and be more consistent with my timing.

"The two cues work together: Rein to bend. Leg to move. I needed to remember to release both cues immediately when the horse yielded.

"Smacks wanted to hang out at the gate. So, Clinton had me do this exercise right in front of the gate, making it a less desirable place for my horse to be.

"Rhythm is still a major concern. When cueing, I have to remember to start with low energy, go to medium, and then move to high. I have to give him a chance to succeed.

"The more we bent and softened, the lower Smacks held his head, and the more balanced he got. He also got out of the habit of snaking his head out and grabbing the reins out of my hand. Every time he acted like he was even thinking of trying to rip the reins out of my hand, we just did a few more minutes of bending.

"I can't believe what a nice canter Smacks has now. He also has quick, correct departures, without throwing himself forward. He is calm and mannerly—after less than a week. It is just amazing!"

❋ *Paula*

"I had to work at not Bending Fancy so quickly, like I was snatching her face off. I also needed to be reminded to release as soon as she softened

"I used spurs on Fancy for this exercise. She was so stiff and unyielding. She was ignoring my cues. Clinton had to *make* me use them. I didn't want to at first. He reminded me that spurs aren't nuclear weapons. I just gently rolled the spurs against Fancy's side. They helped make my cues very specific. They woke her up and made her much more willing to listen to the earlier, subtle cues.

"If she had her way, Fancy would plod along. Clinton told me not to let her walk too slowly when Bending. Moving forward with a little more energy actually made it easier for her to do the exercise well."

Yielding the Hindquarters

9.15

Yielding the Hindquarters allows the rider to direct the horse's power and impulsion.

IMPORTANT NOTE

....

The horse should master **Disengage the Hindquarters** *(p. 60) and* **Flexing Under Saddle** *(p. 137) before learning this exercise.*

Goal

To have the horse pivot around his forequarters, moving his hindquarters away from light leg pressure.

Why Do It?

The horse's power comes from his hindquarters. Gaining control over the hindquarters sets the foundation for teaching lead departures, lead changes, rollbacks and more. *Stage Two—Yielding the Hindquarters Along the Fence* also teaches the horse to move his body laterally and prepares him for learning to sidepass.

As any Australian horseman can tell you, *Yielding the Hindquarters* is essential to a working horse's training. In addition to enabling the horse to perform various maneuvers correctly, on a practical level, Yielding the Hindquarters makes it much easier for a rider to open and shut gates while staying mounted.

9.16
Bring your inside leg back by the horse's flank to cue for the disengage.

Stage One—Disengage the Hindquarters Under Saddle

Teaching Steps

1. Follow Steps 1 and 2 for *Flexing Under Saddle* (p. 137).
2. After picking up the inside rein and pulling it to your hip, put your inside leg back by the horse's flank (fig. 9.16). Look back at your leg. If the horse does not respond to leg pressure alone, gently roll your spur up his side or spank him rhythmically with the end of the mecate.
3. As soon as the horse takes two good steps across with his hind legs, release your leg cue. When the horse stops his feet, flexes his neck, and softens to the rein pressure, immediately drop the rein from your hand.
4. Work on one side until the horse understands what you want, then teach the other side.

Common Rider Mistakes

• Not pulling the rein short enough. If the rein is too long, the horse will have a tendency to walk forward. The more his neck is bent, the easier it is for him to move his hindquarters when you ask.

Looking at your leg helps you bring it back far enough and distributes your weight most effectively.

• Cueing with the leg too far forward. Moving your leg back by the horse's flank (behind the back cinch on a Western saddle) helps to exaggerate your cue and clearly identifies what body part you want the horse to move (fig. 9.17).

• Releasing the rein pressure when releasing leg pressure. Release your leg cue when the horse moves his hindquarters. Don't release the rein pressure until the horse stops his feet and softens his head.

Common Horse Problems

• Walking forward in a circle. Shorten your inside rein more and pull it to your hip. This will discourage forward movement.

• Anticipating the leg cue. If the horse moves before you put your leg on him, spend some time reviewing Flexing Under Saddle (p. 137). This is especially helpful if you have a hotter, more nervous horse.

• Bracing the head and neck or lifting the head in the air. After the horse yields the hindquarters, it is important to wait until he stops and softens his head before releasing the rein pressure. Once the horse understands that he gets rewarded for yielding to the bit, the resistance will go away.

Troubleshooting

- If you have difficulty anchoring the rein hand on your hip, hook your thumb into your pocket to help keep the hand in place.
- If you have trouble using the end of the mecate to spank the horse, use a dressage whip to tap behind your leg and encourage the horse to move his hindquarters.

Tips for Success

- If the horse doesn't seem to understand this exercise, review *Disengage the Hindquarters* (p. 60).

❋ *Cecelia*

"Smacks anticipates. He would start turning before I put my leg on him. We had to review the Flexing exercises for a bit so he could make a clear distinction between the cues. We worked on one side at a time, rather than alternating from side-to-side.

"Putting your leg in the middle of the horse's side is a mixed signal. If the horse walks forward in a circle, make sure that your leg cue is back far enough.

"When I stopped cueing with my leg, Clinton made sure I would hang it down straight. At first, I exaggerated the relaxing cue just as I exaggerated the turning cue to make it as obvious as possible for my horse."

❋ *Paula*

"Fancy got a little cranky when we started this. I had to really roll the spur on her and shorten up the rein. She wanted to walk forward instead of disengaging her hindquarters correctly.

"At first, I had a hard time feeling the hindquarters disengaging. I had to pull up a little harder on the rein and exaggerate the cue more until I felt her step under herself.

"Now I am not at all afraid of what the horse can do. It is *such* a great feeling. I have a whole mental toolbox full of things to pull out and use if I feel like I am losing control."

Stage Two—Yield the Hindquarters Along the Fence

Teaching Steps

1. Walk your horse along the fence line. Hold the middle of the reins with your inside hand.
2. Pick up the outside rein and tip the horse's nose into the fence. At the same time, put your outside leg back toward the horse's flank. Look back at your leg. Yield the horse's hindquarters until the horse faces the fence (figs. 9.18 A & B).
3. Release rein and leg cues. Allow the horse to briefly stand and relax. Walk the horse off again in the same direction. After several strides, repeat the exercise.
4. Do two laps of the arena before changing directions and teaching the horse to yield his hindquarters on the other side.

Common Rider Mistakes

- Pulling the horse's head too much. Pulling too hard on the outside rein when you yield the hindquarters will cause the horse to change directions. Your leg—not the rein—cues the hindquarters to move.

IMPORTANT NOTE
·········
Be sure that the horse has mastered **Stage One** *and* **Follow the Fence** *(p. 150) before teaching this exercise.*

9.18 A & B

Disengage the hindquarters so the horse faces the fence.

Allow the horse a brief rest before continuing the exercise.

• Cueing with the leg too far forward. Exaggerate to teach. Cue with your leg *behind* where the flank cinch on a Western saddle would be. The further back you put your leg, the easier it is for the hindquarters to move.

• Riding too far off the fence. The success of this exercise depends on you staying close to the fence. If you don't, when you cue for the yield, the horse can bring his front end through, rather than moving his hindquarters away.

• Cueing with the rein before moving the leg. Apply both cues simultaneously. The horse should associate moving the hindquarters with the leg cue rather than with the rein cue.

Common Horse Problems

- Not yielding well. Bend the horse's neck more and place your cueing leg farther back. If the horse ignores your leg cue, tap behind your leg with a dressage whip to move him over.

- Backing away from the fence. If necessary, review the *Follow the Fence* exercise. Only allow the horse to rest while next to the fence—not away from it.

- Yielding more than 90 degrees. In the beginning, over-yielding is fine. It is better to have the horse put in a little extra effort to move off your leg rather than ignoring your cues.

Troubleshooting

- If the dressage whip makes your horse jumpy, spend some time rubbing him and desensitizing him to it. He should learn that the whip will never make him feel uncomfortable if he listens and tries.

- Walk a minimum of 15 feet between yields. If the horse anticipates yielding while walking along the fence, walk a bit longer between practicing this exercise.

Tips for Success

- If necessary, to cue correctly, take your foot out of the stirrup. Keep the leg cue exaggerated. As your horse gets more responsive, begin moving the cue forward, little by little.

- It is helpful to use a dressage whip for this exercise because it allows you to cue behind your leg while keeping both hands on the reins.

❈ *Cecelia*

"Remember to put the leg *way* back and exaggerate the cue. Look back at your leg. It gives you a visual cue and helps put your body in the correct position.

"With this exercise, I finally got to hold the reins with both hands. I really needed to be careful, however, not to revert to my old habits. I was still only to use one rein at a time. I had a tendency to pick up contact with my horse's mouth and had to remind myself not to.

"At first, I pulled Smacks' whole head toward the fence. Clinton told me to use the rein only to tip Smacks' nose in the right direction. Tipping his nose to the outside and pushing his hindquarters away with my leg made it easy for him to make the right decision. Again, I was making him responsible for his actions."

❈ *Paula*

"When Fancy didn't want to get off my leg, I just rolled the spur along her side. That was all it took. No more problem.

"We worked hard at staying *right on* the fence. Clinton would yell if we got too far away from it.

"It helped for me to take my foot completely out of the stirrup and cue. That got a much better response until Fancy became completely sure of what I wanted. Looking back at my leg also helped. It turned my body and helped me get into position.

"When Fancy faced the fence, I didn't release the outside rein quickly enough, at first. After she turned her hindquarters, she would back up.

"Don't cue with the leg before tipping the horse's head. Clinton was very clear about the need to do both cues at the same time."

Three Impulsion Exercises

If you can't control your horse's speed, you will spend every ride constantly fighting with him. When mustering cattle in Australia, which meant riding for many miles and many hours at a time, I learned the importance of not micro-managing the horse when we needed to get to work.

These exercises were developed to teach a horse how to control his speed without much interference from his rider. They encourage hot, nervous horses to slow down and relax. They also motivate lazy, disrespectful horses to be more energetic and willing.

Post-to-Post

IMPORTANT NOTE
••••••••
*Before doing this exercise, you and your horse should first master **Bending** (p. 155) and **Follow the Fence** (p. 150). Teach this exercise in an enclosed area. The fence you use should be stable, non-electrified, and high enough to discourage the horse from jumping it.*

Goal

To focus on an object, ride straight to it, and have your horse stop in front of it.

Why Do It?

Post-to-Post teaches your horse to move in a straight line without anticipating whether to go left or right. Stopping at your destination teaches the horse that left and right are not the only options. It helps riders learn to focus on where they need to go.

Teaching Steps

1. Locate a specific fence post on the other side of the arena.
2. Hold the reins in two hands, but keep the reins loose. Trot straight to the post you chose. Post at the trot. Use only one rein at a time for steering.
3. When you reach your goal, sit deep and relax in the saddle. Let your horse stop in front of the post. After a brief rest, bend your horse in a few circles. Repeat the exercise.

Common Rider Mistakes

• Pulling on the reins to stop. Use only one rein at a time to keep the horse straight. Let your chosen post stop the horse's forward motion. If you pull both reins, you only encourage the horse to pull against you.

• Not looking at your destination. No matter how much your horse swerves, keep your eyes on your chosen post.

Common Horse Problems

• Speeding up. If the horse wants to speed up, let him. He will soon realize that he goes nowhere fast. Do not pull back on both reins. If you are afraid of losing control, do a few *Bending* exercises.

• Slowing down before reaching the post. In the early stages, it is all right to let the horse just "dribble down" to a stop at your goal. The more he understands the exercise, the more consistency of gait you can expect.

Troubleshooting

• If your horse weaves badly along the straight lines, you may not have a good "gas pedal." Spend some time reviewing *Cruising* (p. 144).

Pull only one rein at a time to steer. Let the fence stop the horse.

Tips for Success

- Be patient and consistent. At first, you might have to redirect your horse every stride along the straight line. Remember to leave him alone when he goes straight.

❋ *Cecelia*

"Smacks had too much energy. Post-to-Post slowed him down and got him more relaxed in a very short amount of time.

"Clinton stressed how important it is to use each rein independently—never together—on this exercise."

❋ *Paula*

"It was amazing to see how these exercises affected our horses differently. After doing Post-to-Post, Fancy sped up and got more alert. It really helped her to perk up."

Circle at Post

IMPORTANT NOTE
....

*Do not teach this exercise until you and your horse have mastered **Post-to-Post**.*

Goal

To choose an object, ride straight to it, and circle in front of it with no resistance from your horse.

Why Do It?

Circle at Post continues to improve your horse's movement in straight lines. It also reduces the anticipation of going left or right.

Circling at the object improves your horse's softness and bend. It aids in getting him to yield to your leg.

This is an especially good exercise for hot or nervous horses that have a tendency to want to go fast. When they get where they are going, they learn that they have to do a bit more work.

Teaching Steps

1. Choose an object such as a fence post, barrel, or tree some distance away.
2. Hold the reins loosely in two hands. Keep your eyes on your goal and trot straight to the object. Post at the trot.
3. Three strides before you reach your goal, sit the trot. Determine what direction your horse anticipates turning. Plan to go the opposite direction. Apply what will be your inside leg to the horse's side. Bend the horse in a circle in front of your original goal (fig. 9.20).
4. After a few circles, choose another object to ride to and repeat the exercise.
5. After you and your horse have mastered the exercise, canter the lines straight to the object and circle at a sitting trot (fig. 9.21).

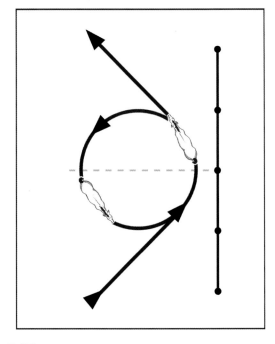

9.20
A straight line extending from the object you chose should bisect your circle.

Common Rider Mistakes

• Stopping at the goal. In this exercise, the horse's feet don't stop. The straight line changes to the circle in one continuous motion. Moving the horse off your inside leg a few strides before you reach the goal helps make a smooth transition from the straight line to the circle.

• Asking for too much bend. The horse's nose should tip slightly to the inside. Bend him only enough to see his inside eye.

• Taking your eyes off the post. Staying focused on your original goal gives you a greater chance of making your circle even and round.

As your horse arcs around in a circle, keep your eyes on the chosen post.

Common Horse Problems

• Speeding up. Don't correct your horse as long as he is under control. When he realizes the other end of the line contains a circle, he won't be in such a hurry to get there.

Troubleshooting

• If your horse has a strong "magnet" pulling him to one spot in the arena, do a lot of circles at that spot. Rest him on the other side of the arena. Repeat this exercise until the "magnet spot" loses its appeal.

Tips for Success

• Keep things interesting. Choose barrels, trees, cars, rocks, or tufts of grass to ride to and circle in front of. Avoid riding your horse to the same spots, time after time.

• Post on the straight lines and sit while circling. Posting will help your balance and is less wearing on your horse's back. Sitting for the circle helps to signal the horse to slow down and wait for a change of cues. Sitting all the time makes it more difficult for the horse to read your cues in the teaching phase because your body language never changes.

Bend the horse around your inside leg. Looking at your chosen post provides a consistent reference point.

- Keep your eyes on your goal the entire time—even while circling. This will help keep your circle balanced and round.

❈ Cecelia

"When circling, I really had to keep my eyes on the post I had chosen. It helped me to envision 'make a small circle at the post' like 'circle at C' in dressage.

"It was a challenge not to keep steady pressure on the inside rein. I had to remember to pull and release, pull and release. If you use steady pressure on the inside rein, you will pull the horse off balance and he will turn too soon.

"Your outside leg keeps your horse from veering too far to the outside of the circle. There is a lot to remember and apply on this exercise."

❈ Paula

"I had to learn not to pull too much if Fancy's head was already turned. I had a tendency to set my hand on my hip, which asked her to stop her feet and flex, instead of walk forward and bend.

"Clinton stressed that I want my horse bending in the circle. Bending means forward movement. I have to remember to release, then pull, then release."

Four Leaf Clover

Goal

To guide your horse in a pattern of straight lines and gentle curves at a consistent gait, meeting with no resistance.

Why Do It?

Four Leaf Clover combines teaching your horse to do smooth, round corners and straight lines. It gets him comfortable being guided around the arena. It is useful for horses that tend to get "ring sour" and who don't want to come off the rail.

The Four Leaf Clover is very effective for teaching your horse to maintain a desired gait during frequent changes of direction. It builds balance and encourages the horse to pay closer attention to his rider.

Teaching Steps

1. Hold the reins in both hands. Reins should be loose and have no contact with the horse's mouth. Ask the horse to trot to the left (counterclockwise) along the perimeter of the arena. Post the trot.
2. At the midpoint of one side, turn left, toward the center of the arena. Ride straight toward the opposite side. Keep the center marker on your left as you pass it.
3. As you near the fence, look left. Turn left. Follow the rail until you reach the midpoint of the next side. Turn left, toward the center of the arena. Ride straight toward the opposite fence. Keep the center marker on your left as you pass by (fig. 9.23).
4. Continue the pattern. At the fence, turn left and follow the rail until the mid-point of the next side. Then turn left and ride straight to the opposite side of the arena.
5. After 10 to 15 minutes, let your horse stop at the center marker. Let your horse rest for five minutes. Then, do the Four Leaf Clover tracking to the right (clockwise).
6. When you and your horse have mastered this exercise, change directions at random. As you trot down the centerline toward the opposite side of the arena, try to feel which way your horse is inclined to go, then turn the opposite way.
7. After mastering this exercise at a trot, do it at a canter. Don't worry about the correct lead, at first. Concentrate on keeping your lines straight and your corners round.

Common Rider Mistakes

• Over-steering or neck-reining. Put pressure on only one rein at a time to keep the horse on the pattern. Otherwise, leave the reins loose.

• "Pushing" the horse into the corners. If the horse starts to cut the corners, resist the temptation to use your inside leg to push him back on the rail. Use your outside rein to bring the horse back to the fence. Make him responsible for staying there.

• Looking down. Concentrate on where you are going. Looking ahead helps keep you balanced and makes your direction cues more specific.

• Passing on the wrong side of the center. When doing a clockwise pattern, keep the center marker on your right. When tracking counterclockwise, keep it on your left. This will help you make straighter lines across the arena. It also helps remind you which direction you will turn.

IMPORTANT NOTE
••••••••

Before beginning, place an orange cone or an upside-down bucket in the center of the arena. This marks the center of your pattern. When working the pattern to the right (making clockwise turns), keep the marker on your right as you pass. When working to the left (counterclockwise), keep the marker on your left. Do not teach this exercise until you and your horse have mastered **Follow the Fence** *(p. 150) and* **Circle at Post** *(p. 168).*

Tracking left. Think of this pattern as a giant "+" sign dividing the arena into four quadrants. An "arc" around each corner connects one leg of the "+" to another leg. You will always turn at the mid-point of a side— never at the center marker.

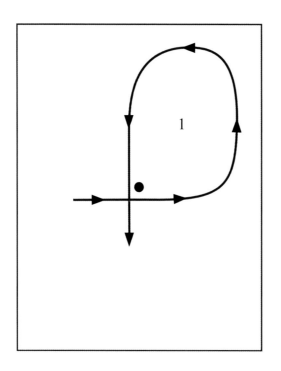

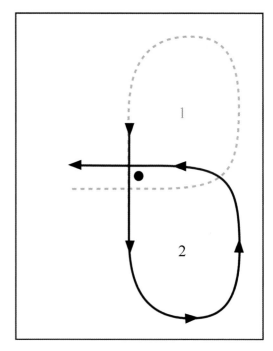

Common Horse Problems

• Anticipating the turns. Some horses try to cut corners or turn too soon, once they understand the pattern. Every time the horse anticipates the turn, go in the opposite direction.

• Speeding up. If you have a hot or nervous horse that wants to speed up, you might tighten up the pattern a bit. It is harder for a horse to go fast when he is constantly turning and changing directions. If the horse breaks gait and canters, bend him in a few circles until he slows down. Then continue the exercise.

Troubleshooting

• If the horse comes too far off the fence on the turns, review *Follow the Fence* (p. 150).

Tips for Success

• Focus on where you want to go. Imagine a carrot dangling on a pole in front of your horse, leading him on. Glue your eyes to that "carrot." Watch where you are going, rather than where you are.

✴ *Cecelia*

"Clinton reminded me that the more wiggly the horse is, the more I must stick to the pattern and not stop to try something else. I wanted to try to set everything up. It was hard to make myself loosen up the reins and make Smacks responsible for himself.

"Clinton told me to dare Smacks to 'run off and be a fruitcake.' My first inclination was to grab onto the reins and try to over-steer. But Smacks can't learn if I am clutching at him. I had to let him make the mistakes so I could correct them.

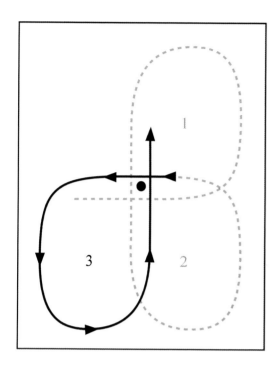 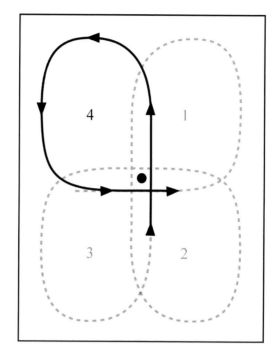

"Keep the marker cone on the left side when doing a left pattern. With so much else to think of, I can't tell you how difficult that was!

"Having the marker cone in the center as a focal point was very useful. I had to remember to look at it each time we turned across the arena. It helped keep my pattern consistent.

"After Smacks understood the pattern, Clinton told me to try to fool him. The key was paying attention to my horse's shoulder—it would tell me which way he planned to go. If I thought he wanted to turn left, I was to turn him right. It didn't take long before he stopped trying to anticipate and began to really listen to me.

"At a canter, we didn't even worry about leads. We only focused on the pattern. Smacks had to figure his leads out on his own. And he did!"

❋ *Paula*

"Remember to look at the center marker after every turn. This exercise helped Fancy's balance—and mine—tremendously!

"At first, our lines were anything but straight. Fancy was like a wiggly, drunk horse. I would really focus on where we were going. As we neared what I was looking at, then I had to remember to refocus on the next destination.

"I like all the exercises. Each one builds on the others and teaches you and your horse something new. For the Four Leaf Clover, I think it would be very helpful to videotape yourself doing the exercise. Then you could go back and analyze what you are doing right and also see what needs work."

Introduction to Sidepassing

Sidepassing combines several cues learned earlier for greater control and enhanced maneuverability.

IMPORTANT NOTE
········

*You and your horse should master **Follow the Fence** (p. 150) and **Yield the Hindquarters Along the Fence** (p. 163) before learning this exercise.*

Goal

To tip the horse's nose to the outside, yield his hindquarters, and sidepass along a fence.

Why Do It?

Sidepassing frees up the horse's front end, ribcage and hindquarters and increases responsiveness to the rider's leg cues.

Sidepassing makes it possible for us to begin working the horse in lateral movements. It aids in teaching the horse collection. When sidepassing, the horse learns to move his feet in a rhythmic, even way, without using his hindquarters for forward impulsion. It teaches a horse to have his shoulders follow his head. Some horses will readily bend their necks, but have a tendency to leave their shoulders behind. Sidepassing helps to correct that problem.

Sidepassing your horse under saddle helps you gain control of his ribcage, shoulders, and hindquarters. Using your legs to steer your horse's ribcage helps you upgrade to "power steering." It helps you maneuver in and out of trees, cattle, or traffic, negotiate tight turns, and make the most of your horse's athletic ability.

Teaching Steps

1. Ask your horse to walk along the rail. Hold the reins with both hands.
2. Tip the horse's nose slightly toward the fence. At the same time, put your outside leg back toward his flank and yield his hindquarters.
3. When the horse has turned perpendicular to the fence, immediately bring your outside leg to the middle of his ribcage and apply pressure. Shift your weight to your outside hip.
4. Point with your inside hand along the fence line. Allow the horse's momentum to carry him sideways. When the horse takes one good step sideways, release all pressure and allow him to stop. Rest five seconds to reward him.
5. Continue walking in the original direction, stopping to sidepass every 10 strides

or so. After two laps of the arena, allow the horse a brief rest. Then teach the sidepass going the other direction.

Common Rider Mistakes

- Dragging the reins across the horse's neck. If the horse doesn't move off your leg, don't try to pull him over with the outside rein. At this stage, always use a direct rein when guiding the horse. Keep your hands at least as wide as your hips.
- Pulling back on the reins. Use the reins only to help give the horse direction. Pulling back on both reins will stop the horse's motion and encourage him to back off the fence.
- Asking for too many steps. Be happy with one good step in the beginning. When you consistently get one good step, ask for two. Quality is more important than quantity.
- Spending too much or too little time on the exercise. When teaching sidepassing, do two laps of the arena in one direction. After a brief rest, do two laps in the other direction. Then work on something else for awhile. Do the exercise long enough for the horse to catch on, but not so long that he becomes bored or frustrated.

Common Horse Problems

- Stopping after yielding the hindquarters. Keep the horse's feet moving. It is much easier to redirect his energy sideways than create that energy from a standstill.
- Lazily yielding the hindquarters. Put your outside leg further back by the horse's flank. Bend his head more toward the fence. The more you bend the horse's neck, the easier it is for the hindquarters to move over.

9.25

Sidepassing to the right. Keep weight in the outside (left) leg. The inside leg is loose, allowing the horse to move sideways.

9.26

Make your cues easy to understand. "Open the door" for the horse with your rein, and push him through with your leg.

- Anticipating the maneuver. If the horse starts to swing his hindquarters away from the fence before you cue, walk longer distances before asking him to yield.

- Not moving off your leg. Use a dressage whip to encourage the horse to move away.

Troubleshooting

- When you release the cueing pressure and allow the horse to stop his sideways motion, make sure he stops perpendicular to the fence.

- If the horse has difficulty understanding this exercise, make it easy for him to find the right answer. Exaggerate your cues. If going to the right, for example, "open the door"—point with your right hand and open your right leg off the horse (fig. 9.26). "Close the door" on the left—hold your left elbow against your belt and your left leg against the horse's side.

Tips for Success

- The fence is your ally in this exercise. Use it to block the horse's ability to go forward. It is much easier for the horse to figure out what you want if he has fewer options.

☀ *Cecelia*

"I like the idea of 'pointing' in the direction you want to go. Throw the 'pick up' rein away when the hindquarters have yielded. Then point in the new direction. The cues are very specific, and you only use one rein at a time. What worked best for me was the concept of 'opening the door' and letting the horse on through.

"Smacks sometimes did more sidepassing than I asked for. But since he was trying, Clinton told me not to pressure him to stop. I just quit cueing—released all leg and rein pressure—until he stopped."

☀ *Paula*

"I had to remember that this was a combination of two exercises. After Fancy faced the fence, I kept forgetting to move my outside leg further forward toward the ribcage to cue for the sidepass.

"I concentrated so hard that Clinton had to remind me to drop my arm when we rested after each sidepass.

"High expectations for this exercise equals doing only one or two steps smoothly and well. It doesn't mean doing a lot of average, sloppy steps."

Vertical Flexion: Poll Control

9.27
Vertical Flexion is important for more advanced collection and impulsion exercises.

IMPORTANT
NOTE
· · · · · · · · ·

*Spend at least two weeks mastering **Flexing** (pp. 91 and 135) and **Bending** (p. 155) before you even think of working on **Poll Control**. Do not rush your horse. Until the horse has learned **lateral flexion**, he will never be ready for **vertical flexion**.*

Goal

To pick up lightly on both reins and have the horse tuck his nose and yield to the bit pressure, creating slack in the reins.

Why Do It?

Vertical Flexion is important when teaching the horse gait extension and collection. It is also essential for teaching advanced maneuvers such as sliding stops, flying lead changes, piaffe, passage, half-pass and others.

When you pick up on the reins and make contact with the horse, he should soften his face and yield at the poll. If the horse resists or throws his head in the air, he loses impulsion and the ability for collection. He also hollows and stiffens his back.

Flexing at the poll enables the horse's hindquarters to come underneath him as well. If you are hunting a fox or chasing a cow, quick stops and tight turns are essential.

It all begins with *Poll Control*.

Teaching Steps

1. Sit on your horse while he stands quietly. Slide your left hand down the left rein until it is about 10 inches from the duct tape.
2. Slide your right hand down the right rein about 10 inches from the duct tape.
3. Pull your left hand to your left leg, just above your knee.
4. Pull your right hand to your right leg, just above your knee. Act as though your hands are glued to your legs.
5. Wait. When the horse keeps his feet still and tucks his nose in—even a tiny bit—instantly open your hands and "throw the reins away." Allow the horse to rest for five seconds. Repeat the exercise (figs. 9.28 A–E).
6. Practice this exercise until the horse immediately tucks his nose in and softens when you pick up on the reins.
7. When you and your horse have mastered Poll Control at a standstill, do it at a walk, trot, and canter. Do not be in a hurry to progress to the next gait. Remember to immediately release the reins when the horse gives to the pressure.

Common Handler Mistakes

- Pulling your hands up in the air. Keep your hands on your legs. The lower your hands, the harder it is for your horse to pull against you. If your hands are in the air, you will have a tendency to pull too hard. You will also have difficulty recognizing the slack in the reins when the horse gives.
- Releasing too slowly. The whole secret to getting your horse light on the bit is the release. When the horse gives, release the reins completely. The quicker you release, the softer the horse will become.
- Using leg pressure. When teaching this exercise at the standstill, there should be no pressure from your legs. Keep your legs hanging and relaxed.
- Releasing the pressure in order to shorten the reins. Releasing pressure always rewards the horse. If you must increase the pressure on the reins in order to be effective, slide your hands along your legs back toward your hips.
- Jerking the reins. Seesawing on the reins will get the horse to tuck his nose in, but it creates a situation where the horse waits for the seesawing motion before he softens.
- Pulling too hard. Don't try to haul the horse's head toward you. You want him to willingly yield to the rein pressure.

Common Horse Problems

- Backing up. Don't make the horse stop backing. Patiently wait until he stops and softens.
- Throwing his head in the air or bracing his head and neck. This behavior is normal in the beginning. Keep your hands set in place. Wait for the horse's feet to stop and for him to soften.

*Slide your hands
down the reins. Pull
your hands to your
hips, one at a time.*

A

B

Wait…When the horse flexes and gives to the pressure, immediately "throw the reins away."

9.29 A & B

When moving forward, take the slack out of the reins. When the horse gives to the pressure, instantly throw the reins away, rewarding him.

- Walking forward. Pull a bit harder on the reins. As soon as the horse stops moving his feet, release the added pressure but maintain the original cue until he yields.
- Nodding. At first, release the rein pressure, even if the horse only nods. When he understands what is expected of him, however, wait until he has committed to yielding before throwing the reins away.

Troubleshooting

- *Do not do this exercise* until all lateral resistance is gone. Most problems arise when people rush to teach Vertical Flexion before the horse is ready.
- If the horse tucks his nose way in toward his chest, but there is still pressure on the reins, you may be pulling too hard. Pick up on the reins until you just make contact. Hold steady, and wait for the horse to soften.

Tips for Success

- "Glue" your hands to your legs when putting pressure on the reins. If your hands move around, you will inadvertently give the horse slight rewards for pulling against you. This will make your cues inconsistent. If your hands remain steady, you will instantly be able to tell when the horse yields to the pressure and will be able to release at the right time.
- Teaching the horse Vertical Flexion creates a new standard and opens a whole new set of rules. From now on, whenever you pick up two reins, don't release until the horse softens. Continue doing most of your riding on a loose rein, making sure your horse is relaxed, soft, and supple laterally. Practice Poll Control a little at each ride until your horse can soften his poll at all three gaits.

✳ *Cecelia*

"Don't take up too much contact—nowhere near as much as for *Bending* or *Flexing to the Bridle*. At first, I made a little too much contact with the reins. I had to remember to start with just a bit, and then ask for more once Smacks started to understand what I wanted."

✳ *Paula*

"Fancy wasn't quite as responsive to the *Flexing* exercises as Clinton would have liked before we started this. He showed me the concept, but told me that I would probably run into some problems because she needed more time to master lateral flexion.

"It is very clear to me that the more time the horse has spent pulling on the owner on the ground, the longer it will take to teach this exercise.

"Fancy eventually did some vertical flexing at a standstill. But it will take a few weeks before she is ready to do this exercise at a walk or a trot."

Backing

Backing helps develop a strong topline and hindquarters.

Goal

To redirect the horse's forward motion into a soft, energetic backup.

Why Do It?

Backing aids in making your horse soft and supple. A good backup helps elevate the horse's shoulders and rounds his back. It is an important part of teaching collection.

Ian Francis, a legendary Australian horse trainer, stressed that my horse would only stop as well as he backed up. Backing is an extension of the stop. If the horse respects the bridle, backs nicely, tucks his head in, and moves lightly off your hand, chances are he will also stop that way. If the horse resists backing, is stiff, and holds his head high in the air, it follows that he doesn't stop very softly, either.

It doesn't matter what riding discipline you prefer, the key to getting great performances out of your horse is developing a soft, energetic backup. The more you develop the horse's hindquarters—the more you have control of them—the better performance your horse will be capable of giving in return.

9.31 A–C

Exaggerate the cue to teach the horse. As soon as he disengages his hindquarters… bring your legs forward and cue him to back up.

Teaching Steps

1. Hold the reins with both hands. From a standstill, yield the horse's hindquarters. When the horse has yielded a few good steps, release the pressure a bit on your inside rein. At the same time, pick up on your outside rein to straighten the horse's head. Move both legs forward (figs. 9.31 A–C).

2. Before the horse's motion stops, "wave" your legs in front of the girth, near his shoulders. If the horse doesn't back up, bump with your legs, one after the other, to encourage his feet to move backward.

3. If the horse still doesn't back up, gently roll your spurs in front of the girth, alternating one, then the other.

4. As soon as the horse takes a couple steps backwards, release all pressure from your

reins and legs and let him rest. Yield the hindquarters in the same direction, and ask the horse to back up again. Yield the hindquarters three to four times in one direction before changing sides.

5. When the horse understands the exercise, ask for more steps backward in a row.

Common Rider Mistakes

• Pulling back on the reins. Though you have gentle pressure on both reins, the goal is not to haul the horse backward. Drive the horse back with your legs. If the horse doesn't back well, use more leg, rather than more rein.

• Asking for too many steps. When teaching your horse, especially one that is resistant, only ask for one or two steps at a time. Don't ask for more steps until he understands what you want.

• Cueing incorrectly with the legs. Cue with the inside leg near the horse's flank to ask the hindquarters to yield. Use both legs, one after the other, in front of the girth to cue him to move backward.

Common Horse Problems

• Stopping after yielding the hindquarters. Cue for the back as soon as you feel the hindquarters yielding energetically. It is much easier for the horse to move backward when his feet already have some energy.

• Putting his head in the air or bracing his neck. At first, ignore this behavior as long as the horse is backing. Once the horse understands the exercise, the head will come down.

• Backing lazily. Your horse may have lazy feet even if he is light on the bit. In this case, yield his hindquarters more aggressively, then redirect that energy backwards while bumping

a little harder with your legs.

• Moving forward. If the horse tries to run forward when you begin using your legs, be sure that you are bumping in front of the girth, near his shoulders. If you cue too far back, the horse will associate that with the cue for going forward. Pull harder on the reins to discourage him from walking forward. When the horse stops moving forward, relax the hands back to a light feel.

• Rearing. Most horses rear because their riders pull too hard on the reins. This can cause them to feel trapped. Use your legs to encourage the horse to go back. Be sure that the combination of your cues isn't forcing the horse to rear.

Troubleshooting

• Don't rush. When you get a few good, light, responsive steps, release all pressure and reward the horse. Don't insist on an energetic, fast backup until he backs well slowly.

Tips for Success

• If your horse resists going backward, review *Backing* from the ground (p. 66). Focus on getting the horse light and responsive.

❋ *Cecelia*

"I had to remember to bend my horse's neck more—to really yield the hindquarters with some impulsion, instead of letting Smacks just take a few lazy steps.

"When yielding the hindquarters, remember to flex first. Then ask for the feet to move. But get ready to cue for Backing before the feet stop from the yielding maneuver. Sometimes Smacks would tuck his head way in, but his feet wouldn't move. To get him to back up, I didn't pull harder; I just used more leg (fig. 9.32).

9.32

Don't worry if your horse is overbent at first. Concentrate on getting his feet moving backward. Use more leg, not more rein.

"Clinton said if Smacks really got stuck, I should do some *Bending* with him and get his feet moving. That did the trick."

✳ *Paula*

"Fancy wanted to run forward. I had to tighten up the rein I used for yielding the hindquarters a little more to stop that tendency. Then she wanted to back up crookedly. Clinton reminded me to keep the rein tension even to cue her for backing straight.

"I forgot to put my feet forward to cue for the backup at first. I also had to remember to let Fancy loose when she backed and not keep the pressure on the reins too long.

"In the beginning, Fancy was a little confused, but it was because she still needed more work at the *Flexing* phase. Clinton showed us what to do, and we did it—to a degree—but he stressed that we should work on perfecting our Flexing and Bending before we spent much time Backing. Once Fancy understood being light to the lateral cues, Clinton said, she would be better able to respond to the backing cues. It took a few days, but focusing on the Flexing did help her Backing."

THE JOURNEY CONTINUES

Where do you go from here?

The lessons in this book provide a solid foundation for whatever riding activities you want to pursue with your horse. Don't be in a hurry. Take the time to master the exercises.

Cecelia and Paula spent a week of concentrated time learning this material. They then went home and continued the training process. Each lady had different goals for her horse. They each had different riding backgrounds and abilities. After learning these exercises, each rider applied them in different ways, depending on the situations they and their horses encountered.

No one can tell you how long it should take to master each lesson. Every rider, every horse, and every situation is different. Progress at a pace that allows you and your horse to succeed. Some days you might teach your horse several new concepts. Other days may be better spent reviewing just one exercise.

I encourage you to enjoy the time spent with your horse. When possible, get out of the sterile arena environment and train in the "real world."

Make contacts with people who share your interests. They can be an invaluable resource, provide encouragement, help troubleshoot, and share successes.

Working with horses is a constant learning process. No one will ever know all there is to know. It is my hope that *Downunder Horsemanship* will not only open up an exciting new world of possibilities for you and your horse, but will also make those new horizons more accessible.

A Final Word from Our Riders

☀ *Cecelia*

"Before we worked with Clinton, I wouldn't regularly canter this horse. I was afraid because

10.1

Expose your horse to new situations. Challenge him to grow in his understanding, respect for you and responsiveness.

10.2

Cecelia and Smacks. "I love that Smacks knows I'm riding him and respects my judgment. It is a fantastic feeling."

I didn't have the tools I needed. Now, I have a whole arsenal of exercises to communicate what I want from him.

"I can't stress enough the importance of the sequential, step-by-step progression of exercises. If you skip anything, it shows up immediately.

"Smacks and I amassed tons of success stories in a very short time after we learned from Clinton. One of the first involved trailering. We spent a week with Clinton without ever coming near a trailer. But when we got ready to leave for home, my horse calmly walked onto the trailer as if he had done it every day of his life! All the *Groundwork Exercises* paid off in spades at that point.

"Shortly after we arrived at home, Smacks and I were returning from a trail ride. We were on the road side when a big dump truck passed us. Smacks became nervous about the situation. Before it got out of hand, I did a *One-Rein Stop*—it worked! He forgot about the scary truck and paid attention to me. We finished our ride safely and quietly.

"On long rides, we often *Cruise* down trails. We even jump fallen trees, 18 inches to two feet in height, with no problems. I just hold his mane and Smacks cruises forward, ears pricked, not rushing or fretting.

"A few weeks after returning home, Smacks and I went on the hound exercises with our hunt club. This is a huge trail ride with over forty fox hounds, six whips and several other horses. We were by a very disobedient horse, but he never bothered us. Every time I thought Smacks was too aggressive in his walk or trot, I would flex him. He never once got out of line. We even led the field at one point. Just as we went into the woods, the hounds broke and the whips fired their pistols. The noise and confusion never fazed him. I was thrilled beyond words!

"After all that, the field waited in a pasture while the whips worked the dog pack on behavior. I flexed Smacks, and then gave him some down time. He stood ever so calmly and quietly while the other new horses jumped and pushed into each other.

"Not long afterward, I took Smacks about fifty miles away to a 'Doubting Thomas' friend's farm. We rode in a big field full of huge, round hay bales. I did the *Circle at Post*

game—cantering from hay bale to hay bale. My friend was shocked that I had so much fun in an open field, doing a relaxed canter on my 'wild' horse, without using the reins. I laughed the whole time. I think Clinton would have approved.

"*No one* can believe the change in my infamous horse. People are overwhelmed by the change in him. At our annual hunt meeting, Smacks and Clinton dominated the conversation.

"Exactly two months after we finished working with Clinton, Smacks and I competed at a dressage show. He scored a very respectable 61.5 and 58.9. He behaved like an aged horse and drew quite a crowd. People who knew him and his history were amazed. They followed us to the arena and gave Smacks a nice round of applause. I couldn't have been happier with his behavior.

"Smacks is stabled at a dressage barn. All the 'dressage queens' love watching the in-hand and under-saddle routine we do before our dressage work. Like me, they now want to do a sliding stop at 'X' in their dressage tests.

"My dressage instructor said she has never seen such a dramatic change in a horse and rider in such a short amount of time. She loves what we did. Sometimes, when Smacks is showing some resistance, she tells me to go back to one of the exercises Clinton had shown us until I get him back on track. Then, the lesson continues. I am so glad to have an instructor who is open to new things.

"I have used what I learned on all of my horses. Every one—from the babies to the seasoned hunters—has benefited.

"Everyone always wants to know the significance of your brand in dressage. I am going to create one in homage to Clinton. It will include a 'Dumbo feather' with a 'CA' worked somewhere in the design. And when people ask what it means, you can bet I'm going to tell them, Clinton Anderson. I credit him for Smacks' success."

✳ *Paula*

"Fancy listens to me much better now.

"When we went to work with Clinton, my horse was very pushy and only green-broke. Now she respects my space. She bucked at the canter before. She never tried that, not even once, when we started these exercises.

"I rode Fancy the night after we came home and she did even better than she did at Clinton's place. I was very impressed. We did every exercise, except *Sidepassing*. I took her down the road a little way, too.

"One night I took her to some friends' and we trail rode. We went through tall grass, over plowed fields, and down a dirt road. She even jumped a creek for me with no hesitation. I was more nervous than she was. The friends could not believe how much both of us have changed! All for the better, of course.

"Here is the best part: I am a cantering fool now! I don't hold the horn when I ride. You don't know what that means to me. I have grown to really like cantering. I never ever thought I would say that.

"Less than three weeks after we came home, I rode Fancy in our town parade. Old tractors were banging, and cars, go-carts, and three-wheelers whizzed around. The only thing that remotely concerned her was a fire-truck horn, blasting about twenty feet from us. Even then, she wasn't bad. The horn startled me more than it did her.

"I have shown some of what we've learned to my 'horse friends.' Some of them have seen bits and pieces from people, but had never had things explained in any particular order. Others had seen different clinicians, but found them confusing or thought they left important information out of their teaching. I stress how one exercise builds on another. When these friends start doing the exercises with their horses, they are amazed at the quick responses.

"About a month after we returned from Clinton's, Fancy acted up a bit. She bucked and tried to run to the barn. It was nothing like she used to do, but it caught me by surprise because I was so used to her behaving well. I know she was just testing me. We went back to *Groundwork Exercises* for a while. It helped get my confidence back and made sure she knew I still deserved her respect.

"Clinton told us about the need for constant maintenance. If Fancy does act up, I have a whole batch of tools that I can use to address the problem. Sometimes we will spend a session just *Cruising* or *Following the Fence*. Some days we focus on groundwork.

"One of the most useful things I have gained from all of these exercises is a better understanding of my horse. I know now when to be firm and when to ease up. I know if she is uptight because I'm rushing her training. When that happens, I back off somewhat and review something I'm sure she knows. Then we try again.

Everyone who knows me knows how much I have valued this whole experience. Thanks to Clinton, I have the kind of horse I have always dreamed of owning."

10.3

Paula and Fancy continue working together. "Now Fancy is the kind of horse I always dreamed of owning."

❊ *Cecelia* thanks:

"Thanks to my husband, Tim, and son, Jake, who encouraged me to do this.

"Thank you, Karen Hayes, the world's greatest friend and groom. Without her, I would have surely died several times over. Her physical and spiritual help made my participation possible and twice as fun!

"Thanks to Deena Smith, my dressage instructor, who got me physically in shape for the intensity of the clinic.

"Thanks to Ami for her encouragement and energy.

"Thank you, Charles Hilton. His smiling face and thumbs up throughout the days lifted my spirits.

"A special thanks to the entire crew who cheered us on each day and helped me dig down for one more exercise!

"Thanks, Smacks, for being a jerk and making the entire experience possible.

"And of course, thank you, Clinton, for having the patience to teach your concepts so thoroughly and generously."

✳ *Paula* thanks:

"First and foremost, thanks to Clinton for choosing me to participate in this project. He gave me something priceless: confidence in my riding and respect from my horse. I am especially grateful he kept working with me until I got things right.

"Thanks to Ami. I have so enjoyed meeting her and working with her on this book project. Thanks for sharing her knowledge and giving advice when I needed it.

"Thanks to Charles for being so nice and taking such awesome pictures. It has been an honor to meet and work with him.

"Thanks to Gale. She made us feel very welcome and has a great upbeat personality.

"Thanks to my husband, Shaun, who has been very supportive on the 'book adventure.' He was such a big help with anything I needed. This is not his hobby—he did it all for me.

Thank you to my sons, Tyler and Cody, for supporting me as I took this trip. They were very happy for me, even though they were without 'mom' for a week. Thanks to them for not burning the house down while we were gone!"

Resources

For Further Study

CLINICS

Participating in a Clinton Anderson clinic is the best way to understand his Downunder Horsemanship® training methods. Each hands-on clinic is limited to fifteen riders and their horses, ensuring that each attendee receives individual attention. Whether they wish to overcome fears, further develop their riding and training skills, gain more control, or build greater respect, clinic participants benefit from Clinton's attention and advice.

To learn about Clinton's current clinic schedule, call (888) AUSSIE-2 [(888) 287-7432]. Observers are always welcome.

TELEVISION

Many trainers and riders have benefited from Clinton Anderson's weekly TV show, *Downunder Horsemanship*® which airs on the RFD-TV network on both DIRECTV and DISH Network satellites. The hour long shows cover a wide range of topics. They feature demonstrations, and Clinton's step-by-step method of training.

The *Lessons with Clinton* episodes feature Cecelia and Paula in action as they learn the various exercises in this book.

In addition, many of the shows are available to own on videotape.

VIDEOS

Clinton offers an extensive video library covering many aspects of riding and training. All training videos demonstrate his step-by-step methods using untrained or "problem" horses. They provide easy to understand instruction that gets quick results. Each is available in VHS or DVD format. Choose from:

Round Penning Series. Learn exercises to help you control your horse off-line in a round pen. Featuring untrained horses as well as novice students.

Gaining Respect and Control on the Ground: Series I (Parts 1 – 4). See Clinton demonstrate *Disengage the Hindquarters, Disengage the Forequarters, Backing, Lungeing—Stage One, Flexing* and *Sending*. You'll also see how to identify and correct common mistakes as you progress in your horse's training.

Gaining Respect and Control on the Ground: Series II (Parts 1 – 4). In these videos, Clinton teaches more advanced exercises such as *Lungeing—Stage Two, Circle Driving,* and *Sidepassing* to refine your ground control. Emphasizing body language and trust building, this series helps you continue improving your communication skills with your horse.

Colt Starting Under Saddle. Join Clinton and Boomerang, a recently captured American Mustang, on this exciting training adventure. See Boomerang's progress through the first two weeks of training, from first touch, to a variety of groundwork exercises, to learning suppleness and responsiveness under saddle.

Riding with Confidence Series I and II. Take your training to the next level. In *Series I*, Clinton demonstrates the *One-Rein Stop*, the verbal "whoa," and teaches a variety of exercises to improve the horse's steering and the rider's independent seat. *Series II* continues to refine the skills learned in *Series I* with advanced riding lessons and training techniques.

No Worries Trailering. Teach your horse to enjoy being in the horse trailer using Clinton's proven loading techniques.

Leads and Lead Changes. For those who have completed the *Ride With Confidence* series, these videos feature Clinton working with trained and untrained horses as he teaches a series of exercises that will take the mystery out of leads and lead changes.

Working with Foals, Weanlings and Yearlings. Learn handling techniques and training methods designed to ensure a lifetime of partnership with your foal. Groundwork exercises geared for a foal's attention span and ability teach respect and build trust, from day one.

Correcting Problems on the Trail. This series addresses every aspect of trail riding so you can make the most of the time spent with your horse. It offers training suggestions for eliminating 15 common problems that can cause trouble on the trail and gives practical safety tips.

Titles and availability subject to change. New titles are released regularly. Contact Downunder Horsemanship® for a complete current listing.

WEBSITE

Visit Clinton's official website, www.clintonanderson.net, for the latest information on upcoming events and appearances, specials, training tips, new video releases, tools and tack recommendations, Downunder Horsemanship® gear, and more!

Glossary

Bending   Turning the horse's head laterally to one side until he yields to pressure, while his feet continue to move his body forward in a small, controlled circle.

Disengage   Moving a specified part of the horse's anatomy sideways to stop forward impulsion.

Downunder Horsemanship®   Clinton Anderson's step-by-step series of training techniques featuring easy-to-understand instruction for quick results. Clinton's training methods based on the philosophy of making the right thing easy and the wrong thing difficult.

Drive Line   An imaginary line where the horse's neck connects to his shoulder. Energy applied behind this line moves the horse forward. The drive line is delineated by tying the string around the horse's neck, just in front of the withers.

Energy   Movement with purpose.

Flexing   Turning the horse's head laterally to one side until his feet stay still and he yields to pressure. Flexing may be done with a halter or in a bridle. Flexing teaches a horse to isolate his head and neck, moving them independently from his body.

Flexion   The act of bending a portion of the neck to respond to pressure. Lateral flexion involves bending the neck from side-to-side. Vertical flexion involves the horse yielding to pressure by relaxing the poll.

Inside   The side of the body closest to the center of a circle. When going clockwise, the *inside* is on the right.

Outside   The side of the body furthest from the center of a circle. When going clockwise, the *outside* is on the left.

Pressure   Energy created by a moving stimulus.

Rhythm   Repetitive movement that may build in intensity but never in speed.

Shades of Gray   Imprecise, erratic or ambivalent cues.

Shank   The first four feet of the lead rope, including the clip.

Softening   Yielding to pressure.

Spanking   Touching the horse with repetitive rhythm, gradually building in intensity until the horse gives the desired response.

Spanker   A short string or rope used in a rhythmic fashion to reinforce an impulsion cue.

Squeezing   Gently closing both legs against the horse's side to cue for impulsion.

Starting Point   The simplest place you can begin training and have the horse understand what is expected.

String   A slim, heavy-duty, six-foot rope used in a variety of ways for desensitizing, as a visual aid, and impulsion.

Tail   1. The part of the lead rope furthest from the clip. 2. The horse's fly swatter.

Yielding   Responding quietly to cues or pressure.

Index